ROOM FOR DESSERT

ROOM FOR DESSERT.
Copyright © 1999 by David Lebovitz.
All rights reserved. Printed in the United
States of America. No part of this book
may be used or reproduced in any
manner whatsoever without written
permission except in the case of brief
quotations embodied in critical articles
and reviews. For information address
HarperCollins Publishers, Inc.,
10 East 53rd Street,
New York, NY 10022.

HarperCollins books may be
purchased for educational, business,
or sales promotional use. For
information please write:
Special Markets Department,
HarperCollins Publishers, Inc.,
10 East 53rd Street,
New York, NY 10022.

FIRST EDITION

Designed by Vertigo Design

Photography by Michael Lamotte

Art direction and prop styling by
Sara Slavin

Food styling by David Lebovitz

Library of Congress
Cataloging-in-Publication Data
Lebovitz, David.
    Room for dessert : 110 recipes for
cakes, custards, soufflés, tarts, pies,
cobblers, sorbets, ice creams, cookies,
candies, and cordials / David
Lebovitz.—1st ed.
        p.   cm.
Includes bibliographical references and
index.
ISBN 0-06-019185-6
1. Desserts. I. Title
TX773.L385   1999
641.8–DC21   99-17078

99 00 01 02 03 RRD 10 9 8 7 6 5 4 3 2 1

110 RECIPES FOR
CAKES, CUSTARDS,
SOUFFLÉS, TARTS,
PIES, COBBLERS,
SORBETS, ICE CREAMS,
COOKIES, CANDIES,
AND CORDIALS

HarperCollins*Publishers*

ROOM FOR
DESSERT

DAVID LEBOVITZ

FOREWORD BY ALICE WATERS

PHOTOGRAPHY BY MICHAEL LAMOTTE

CONT

ESSENTIALS

CAKES

CUSTARDS AND SOUFFLÉS

FRUIT DESSERTS

SORBETS, SHERBETS, ICE CREAMS, AND GELÉES

COOKIES AND CANDIES

LIQUEURS AND PRESERVES

BASICS

FOREWORD

David Lebovitz has a long history at Chez Panisse, where he started out making salads before he was recruited by the pastry chef, my partner Lindsey Shere. The pastry kitchen at Chez Panisse makes an ever-changing array of desserts for the upstairs café, as well as the single dessert served on the fixed-price restaurant menu downstairs, which also changes daily. During the twelve years he worked for us, David soaked up Lindsey's high standards and good judgment and learned her vast dessert repertoire of French and American classics, Italian recipes passed down in her family, and her own improvisations and variations on the themes of simplicity and seasonality. David shone in the pastry kitchen. He was reliable and proficient, and he never lost his sense of humor, even when he had to simultaneously mollify an impatient waiter, keep an eye on cookies in the oven, beat egg whites for a soufflé, and be gracious to the important guest who was dining in the kitchen—and taking up what little room there was left to maneuver in.

However, David really came into his own at Monsoon, Bruce Cost's beautiful and all-too-short-lived pan-Asian restaurant in San Francisco. On the eve of his opening, Bruce was still desperately seeking a pastry chef, and someone suggested he should try to lure David away from Chez Panisse. Lindsey and I didn't want him to go, but we knew he should—it was a great opportunity. We were both delighted by how creatively he seized it at Monsoon, inventing imaginative desserts that harmonized beautifully with Bruce's eclectic mix of dishes from all across Asia, many of them new and strange to Western palates. David's challenge was to reconcile the Western sweet tooth with Bruce's very authentic cuisine. This he did brilliantly, with subtle and satisfying desserts that were adventurous and sometimes whimsical explorations of tropical Asian ingredients, which he learned to use expertly. I remember meals at Monsoon ending with little tropical fruit soups and keenly flavored sherbets and with seductively spiced cookies and candies—and always just the right amount of restraint.

When I think about David's desserts, I'm reminded of a trip I once took to Japan, where I was a guest at an exquisite *kaiseki* meal that drew to a close with a memorable dessert: a perfect glass of tangerine juice, freshly squeezed from the ripest, tastiest fruit and served at the perfect temperature—slightly chilled, but not too cold. Dessert should always have that same deliciousness, balance, and inevitability, but it takes someone like David, with real taste buds and real taste, to know how to end a meal without obliterating what came before. Dessert making is not a branch of cooking that usually attracts minimalists, but David is one of those rare pastry chefs who knows that in desserts, as in all art, the cliché is true: sometimes less is more.

David's sense of style has a refreshing modernity to it. In fact, his desserts have a lot in common with the best modern design. They don't have any extraneous ornament, they are not excessively formal, and they have simplicity and clarity. Above all, they proceed from the very first principles of good cooking: Use the best and purest food—local, seasonal ingredients grown by people who are farming organically and sustainably. And make it simple. When you make David's recipes in this book, guided by these same principles, you will be rewarded with desserts that are both irresistible and inspiring.

ALICE WATERS

ACKNOWLEDGMENTS

This cookbook owes its existence to many people. To the following, to whom I am particularly grateful, my deepest thanks:

Lindsey Shere, one of the founders of Chez Panisse, whom I am lucky to have worked alongside during much of her twenty-five-year tenure as pastry chef. Lindsey always encouraged me to taste new things and try new techniques. She let me make mistakes, and she taught me how to learn from them. She was as generous with her wisdom about life as she was with her wisdom about cooking.

Lindsey's partner Alice Waters, who taught me what cooking is really about. She constantly pushed me to pursue the finest, freshest ingredients in order to capture and appreciate their flavors for what they are. Alice taught me that "just okay" is never good enough—and that making it simple is usually best.

Fritz Streiff, another longtime Chez Panisse colleague, who helped me put together recipes and thoughts for this book so that it would reflect my passion for making desserts—and eating them! Throughout the entire project, Fritz has shared my enthusiasm and perfectionism, and he has happily tasted almost everything in this book.

Coworkers from the Chez Panisse pastry department, past and present, who over the years have shared ideas, inspiration, and knowledge: John Luther, Otto, Hye Paik, Charlene Reis, Lisa Saltzman, Shari Saunders, Alan Tangren, Anthony Tassinello, Bridget Venus, Diane Wegner, and Samantha Wood. Special thanks to Linda Zagula, a paragon of good humor and a general whiz in the kitchen, and to Mary Jo Thoresen, a wonderful pastry chef and the best of friends.

Bruce Cost, Marion Cunningham, Doralece Dullaghan, Bill Fujimoto, Tony Gulisano, Rochelle Huppin-Fleck, Julie Jordan, Nick Malgieri, Alice Medrich, Patricia Rain, Shirley Sarvis, John Scharffenberger, Nancy Silverton, Peggy Smith, Robert Steinberg, Kathleen Stewart, and Joanne Weir: all baking and food friends who have advised and encouraged me.

Flo Braker, not only the greatest baker but a great friend, and the only person I know who can make tiny taste terrific. For her willingness to share her knowledge and experience with me, and for her constant and unending support for everything I've ever done, including this book, I owe her enormous, inexpressible gratitude. Thanks, Flo!

My wonderful agent, Fred Hill, who spotted a sliver of hope in my modest proposal, and my editor, Susan Friedland, who had the patience to take a rookie under her wing.

The staff at HarperCollins who all did a remarkable job: assistant editor Ellen Morrissey, who graciously took care of the details and changes; copy editor Estelle Laurence; and production editor Christine Tanigawa.

Michael Lamotte, Sara Slavin, and Bill Checkvala, whose extraordinary artistic photography and art direction helped create the look of this book.

Chez Panisse, Clifford Colvin, Fillamento, Heath Ceramics, Tim Montesonti, Naomi's, Scharffen Berger Chocolate, Lindsey Shere, Sur La Table, Zinc Details, and above all, Centrium Furnishings, for their generous loan of props.

Lynn Brei, Jodi Caruna, Scott Enderby, Alan Linder, and Jeff Louie, who tested these recipes to make sure they would work in home kitchens.

Kip Turnquist, whose friendship has been warm and heartfelt and who has shared many unforgettable times with me.

And finally, Fred Lech, for his support and encouragement while I worked on this book; and for never once complaining about the overstuffed refrigerator and freezer, the cakes and cookies piled high on the counters, and the stacks of recipe notes everywhere; and for gladly eating everything I made—even the stuff with ginger in it.

INTRODUCTION

The very first dessert I can remember making was a bowl of blackberries. In the woods surrounding my childhood home in New England were thickets of blackberry bushes, with shiny dark berries clinging to thorny branches. My sister and I were always so excited when we picked them that we would disregard the thorns. Then we would run home, all scratched up and exhilarated, having already eaten more than half of what we had picked. And instead of further delaying our gratification by making a pie or cobbler, we divided the berries into bowls and ate the rest. If I was dividing them I was sure to be extra generous with mine—so long as no one was paying attention. A topping of thick, tangy sour cream and a sprinkle of sugar, a few turns with our spoons, and we called it dessert.

My culinary training has not been traditional. I didn't go to culinary school. I didn't do an internship. I went to film school and learned to look at the world through a lens, developing an eye intent on purifying and simplifying. Then I started applying the same aesthetic to food. The first place I cooked was a popular and very ambitious natural food restaurant in my college town where everything was made from scratch, including bread and ice cream. At the Cabbagetown Café, we cooked and baked without food processors or mixers or kneading machines, because the owner, Julie Jordan, insisted, quite correctly, that machines would keep us from directly experiencing our ingredients. At the Cabbagetown, these ingredients included fruits and vegetables we were able to buy directly from local growers, people we could talk to and learn from.

Then I spent a year touring Europe, eating my way through every country on the Continent. While other people were visiting cathedrals and museums, I was crisscrossing the cities and countryside by foot, public transit, and thumb, looking for the best bakeries and pastry shops.

When the *Chez Panisse Menu Cookbook* was published, I kept it next to my bed, reading parts of it over and over. I was in love with just about every recipe and idea in the book, especially the idea of a restaurant where the menu was constantly changing, using only the most beautiful and flavorful regional ingredients. I knew I had to work there. As John Thorne wrote years later, in his newsletter *Simple Cooking*, "Chez Panisse was the one French restaurant that didn't make you want to go to France: it made you want to move to California." So I moved to California, and soon I was cooking in the café upstairs at Chez Panisse.

Eating at the Chez Panisse café in those days was a lot like attending a fascinating, noisy, informal dinner party. Sometimes I wonder how we turned out such simple but fabulous food, night after night, with the volume turned up so high. These were some of the most hectic, frenzied times of my life, but they were undoubtedly the most fun. I was put to work at the salad station, where I learned to make salads by letting the greens arrange themselves naturally, falling from my fingers into a leafy pile on the plate. The ingredients were always allowed to speak for themselves.

In the café's open kitchen, just a few feet away from where I made salads, stood the display of pastries. Of course, these were not ordinary desserts, but desserts by Lindsey Shere, one of the founders and owners. Every night the display was different. Usually there were rustic-looking almond tarts, with a caramelized texture that managed to be crisp and chewy at the same time. Sometimes there was a rich chocolate cake sitting proudly atop a hammered-copper cake stand, waiting to be sliced and served with swirls of ever-so-gently whipped cream. In season, there were Bosc pears, an astonishingly brilliant red, poached in Zinfandel. Often there were creamy custards in earthenware ramekins, topped with a sprinkle of fresh candied citrus zest. Almost always, simple fruit tarts, buttery pastry encasing the most luscious fruits I'd ever seen.

I spent many of my evenings at work pestering the pastry people with queries about doughs, flours, sugars, fruits—anything that had to do with the pastry kitchen. (Now I can apologize publicly to all the people who may have had to wait for their salads while I quizzed the dessert cooks!) In my spare time, I studied dessert cookbooks and practiced. Just when I feared that they had all had enough of me and my questions, Lindsey offered me a position in the pastry department. I learned later that Mary Jo Thoresen, one of the pastry cooks, had been sufficiently impressed by my salads—and by my persistence and curiosity—to insist to Lindsey that I immediately be recruited to make desserts.

I worked in the pastry department at Chez Panisse in Berkeley about twelve years in all. Lindsey taught me about perfect fruits and sweet and tangy berries and then she turned me loose. I made dark bittersweet chocolate cakes with espresso crème anglaise, peaches and nectarines in warm tartlets with freshly churned vanilla ice cream, and sherbets that were the essence of the fruit themselves, served with a buttery assortment of sugar cookies.

Desserts were never extravagantly or elaborately decorated at Chez Panisse. I remember saying to Lindsey once that I regretted never having learned all the fancy pastry decorating skills. She answered, "But why? Most of that stuff really doesn't taste very good, you know." Instead, from Lindsey and Alice I learned how to pick out a ripe peach, how to get to know your sources and how to trust them, and how to tell the difference between what's really good to eat and what's not. In short, Chez Panisse taught me how to express the simple beauty of food.

My years at Chez Panisse were interrupted only once, when I was invited to be the pastry chef at Monsoon, a San Francisco restaurant that became a huge critical success during its three-year existence. Monsoon was owned by Bruce Cost, the most scholarly chef I've ever met. Bruce had become thoroughly versed in the traditional cuisines of China and Southeast Asia, and all his dishes were prepared with great authenticity and care. I loved the first and only dessert Bruce Cost ever made for me: a quartered pear sautéed with brown slab sugar, sweet Tientsin black vinegar, ginger slices, and shards of cassia bark. That was it. And it was really good.

My challenge was to create original desserts with a wide variety of Asian ingredients, such as fresh litchis and stinky durian fruit, young coconuts, palm sugar, rock sugar, and Shaoxing and osmanthus blossom wines. Here was a once-in-a-lifetime opportunity to familiarize myself with ingredients that before then I had only wondered about when I spotted them at Asian markets. I was also being deeply influenced by the Asian cooking traditions I was learning, especially the insistence, just as at Chez Panisse, on the absolute freshness of so many ingredients.

At Monsoon, I made desserts like rice tart with mangoes, tropical fruit soup with lemongrass and bitter almond jelly, coconut tapioca pudding, plum wine–blackberry sorbet, and fresh durian cream pie. (After I served this last dish to Alice Waters on one of her visits to Monsoon, she sent me a cryptic note that said only, "How dare you!") It was great fun inventing these treats—and fun for the customers, too, since no one else at the time was concocting desserts anything like these. Many recipes in this book originate from my experimentation at Monsoon, and I hope they inspire you to do some experimenting of your own.

When I was choosing recipes to put into this book, I had two major criteria: the ingredients had to be accessible, and the recipes had to be easy to duplicate in the average home kitchen. I left out a lot of recipes because they included steps that belong to the category of Things Nobody Wants to Do at Home: tempering chocolate, for example, or spinning sugar, or decorating anything with more than one pastry bag! I left out others because they had too many steps. I love to eat and I hate to wait too long for an outcome, so I tend to favor recipes that are relatively easy.

Even my more complicated recipes are not so daunting when you realize that many of the elements of these desserts can be made in advance. For the Meyer lemon semifreddo (page 40), for example, the sponge cake can be made several days in advance, the lemon curd can be made up to a week ahead, and the final assembly will take less than an hour. Even a soufflé, that icon of fancy dessert making, is really a very simple proposition: The pastry cream base can be made the day before, and all you will have to do at mealtime is beat egg whites, fold them into the base, and bake.

All the recipes in this book are about flavor first and how to show off the ingredients: perfectly ripened fruit, freshly ground spices and toasted nuts, caramel so dark it's nearly burnt, bittersweet chocolate so intense it screams Chocolate!

A chocolate cake should always have that screaming chocolate intensity. A lemon dessert should always sparkle with that clean citrus tartness that is so appealing after dinner. Sauces should complement flavors, not compete with them. I want things to taste good together, not jerk your palate around in different directions—for example, I don't like most desserts that combine fruits and chocolate: The flavors are all over the place.

Shapes should be clean and interesting. I don't mind decor per se, as long as it's minimal and part of the dessert; but I don't like anything on the plate that I can't devour—and some of these elaborate vertical dessert follies served nowadays have inedible elements: spirals and sharp shards of caramel, for example—ouch! And what's up with those tiny dots of sauce that don't do anything? If a sauce is part of the dessert, I want there to be enough of it, not just a decorative dribble of raspberry sauce purely for show.

When you search out the best ingredients, do as little to them as possible, and serve them in a straightforward way, the presentation follows naturally. A glossy custard looks best with a swirl of whipped cream; a cool tapioca pudding looks enticing when it's accompanied with its natural complements—tropical fruits and shaved coconut.

At Chez Panisse, Alice was constantly insisting that things be simplified. Doing this can be deeply satisfying. I have tried to make the recipes in this book as simple, clear, and easy to follow as I know how. They require no magical techniques, no elaborate equipment, and no impossible-to-find ingredients. I hope that you will make the recipes in this book often, and that at least a few of them will become part of your standard repertoire, too, as you re-create your favorites over and over.

ESSENTIALS

EQUIPMENT

After spending years in restaurant kitchens, I began to notice that whenever I made desserts at home, it always seemed to take a lot longer to do things than it did at work. Then I realized that I needed to set up my home kitchen more or less like a professional pastry kitchen. That didn't necessarily mean buying only the most expensive cookware and every conceivable gadget, but it meant organizing and outfitting my home kitchen so that tools were within easy reach, ingredients were stored in convenient plastic bins, and the cookware was heavy-duty and durable. Baking is much more enjoyable if you use well-selected, top-quality equipment—the work goes faster and, best of all, you get better results.

Electric Mixer: A good sturdy countertop mixer is likely to be your most worthwhile expense for baking. I use a KitchenAid K5. An extra stainless steel bowl is invaluable if you bake a lot. I also recommend buying an extra paddle and whip, which will save you the trouble of scrambling to wash and dry them midway through a recipe. If you don't have room for a standing mixer, I recommend a powerful handheld one.

Food Processor and Blender: I use my food processor for chopping candied citrus peel, grating fresh coconut, and puréeing fruits and berries (I prefer chopping nuts by hand, though). Avoid underpowered machines, which stall and break down. Good brands are Cuisinart and KitchenAid.

I use a blender for puréeing cooked fruits for sorbets and preserves. If you are puréeing something hot, remember to fill the jar no more than halfway, or the hot liquid can shoot out over the top and cause injury.

Food Mill: Food mills make easy work of separating the seeds from the pulp of bushberries such as raspberries and blackberries without cracking the seeds, which causes bitterness. Buy one with interchangeable disks with holes of various sizes. Foley, Rösti, and Mouli all make good food mills.

Measuring Cups and Spoons: I believe in having at least two or three 4-cup and 2-cup measuring cups on hand. Otherwise you'll have to interrupt what you're doing to wash and dry the one you have in order to measure something else. Also essential is a good set of graduated measuring cups for dry ingredients, in ¼- to 1-cup sizes. With a graduated set, measuring dry ingredients is more reliably accurate, since the level edges make it easy to scoop up flour, for example, and sweep away the excess with a straight-edged utensil or the back of a knife—the correct way to measure it.

Mixing Bowls: I like to have lots of these on hand because baking often requires the use of many bowls at the same time. Nested stainless steel bowls are lightweight and durable and they save space. Sur La Table (see Sources, page 205) sells mixing bowls with rubber bases to keep them in place when you are adding ingredients with one hand and whisking or stirring with the other. (You can also dampen a kitchen towel, twist it like a rope, form it into a ring on the counter, and set the bowl in the center to hold it steady.)

Egg whites beaten in a copper bowl have a more stable structure, which results in creamier meringues and smoother soufflés. Always clean a copper bowl before using it by swishing around a small amount of vinegar and salt, rinsing, and drying well.

Plastic Containers: Plastic tubs with airtight lids will keep things fresh. I keep flour, sugar, and nuts in sturdy Cambro containers, which are available at restaurant supply stores and from the King Arthur Flour Company (see Sources, page 204). Tupperware has a wonderful selection of containers, but you'll need to have a party, or go to one! Cookies should always be stored in an airtight container at room temperature.

Baking Dishes: Recipes in this book are mostly scaled for 2-quart baking dishes. This is the right size for most crisps, cobblers, bread puddings, and the like. A large baking dish or roasting pan makes a good water bath for gently baking custards and cakes such as the chocolate orbit cake (page 24). For bread puddings and for chilled trifle-style desserts, I recommend a 2-quart porcelain soufflé dish.

Ladles, Spoons, and Spatulas: I often use heat-resistant rubber spatulas for stirring custard mixtures because their shape and flexibility allow them to reach tight corners in saucepans. For stirring caramel, I prefer a flat-edged wooden spatula. I keep at least five or six spatulas in my kitchen, as well as one or two handheld plastic scrapers. Be sure to smell them before use, since plastic and wood absorb odors and flavors, and you don't want your custards tasting like last night's aïoli. Stainless or wooden spoons are useful, and so is a 1- or 2-ounce ladle for measuring and pouring crêpe batter and for ladling sauces.

Metal Spatulas: Both straight and offset (or angled) metal spatulas are used for decorating and spreading. I have several of both, both small (with 4-inch blades) and large (with 8- and 10-inch blades). A cake lifter, a very wide spatula about 10 inches across, is useful for easily picking up cake layers, whole cakes, and tarts without breaking them. Sur La Table (see Sources, page 205) carries a good selection of these.

Cutting Boards: I recommend plastic cutting boards because they are dishwasher-safe. Whether you use wood or plastic, once a cutting board shows signs of wear, discard it and buy a new one.

Thermometers: Check your oven periodically with a good oven thermometer to be sure the built-in thermostat is accurate, and have it calibrated if it isn't. An instant-read thermometer is useful for checking the temperature of custards, and a candy or jelly thermometer, preferably one with a metal back (the all-glass ones break too easily), is indispensable for making certain candies and preserves. After using a glass thermometer, clean it and store it in a cardboard paper towel tube to prevent breakage.

Pastry Brushes: These are used for applying glazes, buttering cake pans, and brushing cakes to saturate them with flavored syrups. When dough is being rolled, a dry brush will remove excess flour, which could otherwise toughen the pastry. Buy inexpensive soft-bristled brushes at cookware or hardware stores, and discard them when they start losing their bristles.

Rolling Pin: Use whichever kind of rolling pin you prefer—the kind with handles and ball bearings or the kind without, known as a French rolling pin. I prefer a heavy rolling pin with handles because the weight of the pin helps roll out the dough.

Bench Scraper: I wouldn't bake without one. They're great for lifting ingredients, spreading and scraping up chocolate, and scraping countertops and cutting boards.

Cookware: Bad pots and pans are poorly balanced, warp and won't sit flat, and have hot spots. My favorite cookware is made by All-Clad: well-designed, heavy-duty, solid pots and pans with handles that stay cool on the stove top. I recommend an inexpensive starter set.

For frying crêpes, I like the Anolon nonstick pans. They have an extremely durable nonstick coating.

Tart Rings: Also called quiche pans, tart rings are two-piece metal pans with removable bottoms that fit in low rings with scalloped sides. The tart recipes in this book call for 9-inch round tart pans.

Baking Sheets: You should have at least two baking sheets on hand, especially when baking cookies. Standard baking sheets are about 12 by 18 inches, although there is some variation in the sizes of different brands. Avoid using baking sheets that are coated black: they heat too quickly and can cause burnt bottoms on cookies and cakes.

Parchment Paper and Baking Sheet Liners: Using parchment paper to line a pan makes it easy to remove baked cookies or cakes. Rolls of it are sold in any well-stocked supermarket or cookware store. I buy it by the case.

Exopat or Silpat sheets are flexible sheets of a nonstick silicone material strong enough to withstand even the high heat of caramel. They are reusable up to two thousand times and are available at any good cookware store.

Scale: If you do a lot of baking, you'll want a scale sooner or later, since many pastry recipes call for ingredients by weight. Professionals tend to prefer recipes in weights, but you can get by without a scale for most of the recipes in this book since I've given volume equivalents.

Timer: Since timing is critical for most baked goods, especially cookies, I recommend a small digital timer that you can slip in your pocket and keep with you.

Knives: A long, sharp serrated knife with a 12- to 14-inch blade is a must for cutting soft sponge cake and for slicing other cakes horizontally into layers. A high-quality 8-, 10-, or 12-inch chef's knife is also important—whichever size feels right in your hand. A 3- to 4-inch paring knife is necessary for peeling and slicing fruits. The best knives are made of stainless steel; avoid carbon steel, which reacts unappetizingly with fruit acid.

Cake Pans: Most of the cake recipes in this book call for a 9 by 2- or 3-inch cake pan. Shallower ones don't hold enough batter for these cakes. Magic Line pans (available from Parrish, see Sources, page 204) and Ateco pans (from Sweet Celebrations, see Sources, page 205) are both reasonably priced and come in all sizes and shapes.

A 9½-inch springform pan is necessary for delicate cakes that cannot be flipped to be removed from the pan.

Strainer: A stainless steel mesh strainer with a fine screen is adequate for straining custards and infusions. A strainer can also serve double duty as a sieve for mixing and aerating dry ingredients and for dusting cakes with powdered sugar.

Zesters, Graters, and Vegetable Peelers: These are used to remove the colorful and highly flavorful part of the citrus skin that contains the essential oils. I use a zester in most cases, zesting directly into the pan or bowl to collect the oil that sprays as you zest. A stainless steel vegetable peeler will peel off larger strips of skin. The best, sharpest peeler is made by OXO Good Grips. A box grater with four or five sides is useful for grating fresh coconut and its fine-holed side can also be used to grate nutmeg.

Ramekins and Custard Cups: I have both elegant porcelain 4-ounce ramekins and a set of 6-ounce Pyrex custard cups (available at supermarkets and hardware stores). Any ovenproof custard cups are fine for my recipes, which are in 4-ounce servings.

Juicer: I use the juicer attachment on my food processor when I need a lot of juice for a sorbet. Otherwise I use a vintage glass reamer. For the maximum yield of juice, the fruit should be at room temperature; roll it on the counter, pressing down firmly to rupture the juice sacs within before you cut it in two and juice it.

Spice Grinders: Unless you do a lot of spice grinding, use a mortar and pestle for grinding spices. I use a Japanese mortar called a suribachi, an earthenware bowl with an unglazed, deeply combed and ridged interior. You can also dedicate a coffee grinder specifically for spices. Or simply wrap the spices in a few plastic bags and crush them with a hammer or another heavy, blunt object.

For grating fresh ginger, a Japanese ginger grater with tiny sharp teeth works well, removing much of the fiber. If you don't have a ginger grater, peel the ginger, slice it thin with a sharp knife, and chop it with a pinch of salt to help break it up.

Cooling Racks: A good, sturdy cooling rack about 10 by 18 inches is good to have for cooling cakes and baking sheets. The King Arthur Flour Company (see Sources, page 204) sells a rack that holds four baking sheets at once, and folds to less than an inch high for storage.

Whisks: You need at least one wide balloon whisk for whipping anything in a bowl (such as egg whites) and a longer straight whisk for whisking in saucepans. Buy only restaurant-quality whisks; they take being whacked around better than cheaper whisks.

Ice Cream Freezer: If you like ice cream, a quality machine with a self-contained refrigeration unit will be a good purchase. I got mine from Williams-Sonoma (see Sources, page 206). Less costly machines, such as the Krups La Glacière, work well, although they have containers that must be frozen overnight before use.

Pie Plates and Weights: I use mostly 10-inch pie plates. My favorites are heavy glass Pyrex ones, which conduct heat well and allow you to see how your pie is browning on the bottom. You can substitute a 9-inch pie plate for my recipes if you don't have a 10-inch one.

For prebaking pie crusts, the best pie weights are pennies, which are great conductors of heat because of their copper content, and are quite reasonable in price at one cent apiece. You can also used dried beans, rice, or the pie weights available in cookware stores.

INGREDIENTS

Many of the ingredients used for desserts are costly, and therefore you should spend wisely and seek out the best. Great chocolate, for example, costs only slightly more than bad chocolate. Whenever you make a dessert, you want it to show off to its best advantage—and the time and labor you spent making it would be wasted if you used inferior chocolate, or unripe fruit, or stale nuts.

In order to judge the best, here's a short primer on ingredients.

Chocolate: Chocolate recipes in this book call for dark chocolate, either unsweetened or bittersweet. Dark chocolate is an emulsion of roasted cacao beans ground to a paste, to which cocoa butter, emulsifiers, and sugar are sometimes added. The factors that contribute to the final taste and texture of chocolate include the selection and fermentation of the raw cacao beans; their careful roasting and blending; and the grinding, heating, and kneading of the roasted beans. The final step in chocolate manufacture is called "tempering" the chocolate, a process which stabilizes the fat and sugar crystals so that the chocolate will have good texture and snap, and so that no "bloom" of cocoa fat will streak the surface of the finished chocolate. Dark chocolate will keep for several years if it is stored in a cool, dry place (not the refrigerator).

When I call for bittersweet chocolate in this book, you can use any good-quality sweetened dark chocolate labeled "bittersweet" or "semisweet."

When melting chocolate by itself, it is very important that no moisture gets into the chocolate or it will seize and turn into a grainy mass. Check your utensils and bowls and wipe them completely dry before using them. Do not let steam from a neighboring pot or the double boiler get into the chocolate, either. If your chocolate does seize, you can turn it into chocolate sauce by adding some water and cream or butter. Start again with some fresh chocolate—and be more careful.

I use several different chocolates, from both the United States and Belgium. My favorites are Scharffen Berger, Callebaut, and Guittard (see Sources, pages 203–205).

White Chocolate: Buy only white chocolate that contains cocoa butter, sugar, and milk powder. In products labeled "white coating," the flavorful cocoa butter has been replaced with vegetable fat; it's bland and waxy and I don't use it. Because of its perishability, white chocolate should only be purchased in small quantities, or as needed. Lindt, Callebaut, and Valrhona are good brands (see Sources, pages 203–205).

Cocoa: I usually use finely ground Dutch-process cocoa, since it dissolves better in liquids. For chocolate sauce and other recipes where cocoa is added to a liquid, sifting the cocoa and whisking it together with the sugar in the recipe before adding will help disperse the cocoa and prevent lumps from forming.

Espresso: The concentrated flavor of espresso is important in my recipes, so if you don't have an espresso machine, do not substitute coffee. Instead use an instant espresso powder such as Nescafé Espresso Roast instant coffee. This powder is quite strong and is processed in a way that preserves the flavorful coffee oils.

Milk, Cream, and Crème Fraîche: For the purposes of this book, milk means whole milk. For most ice cream, pudding, and custard recipes, you can substitute lower fat, 1 or 2 percent milk; however, the dessert will not have as rich and creamy a texture and flavor as the same dessert made with whole milk. If you must, half-and-half can be substituted for heavy cream in rich custards and ice creams.

I strongly recommend finding a good organic heavy cream that has not been ultrapasteurized, and that has a fresh, sweet cream taste. Keep it well chilled until ready to use. If you are making whipped cream, it's a good idea to chill the bowl and the beaters before whipping the cream.

Crème fraîche is heavy cream that has been cultured, giving it a slight tang and a silky richness. You can make your own crème fraîche by mixing 1 cup of heavy cream with 1 tablespoon of buttermilk or crème fraîche from a previous batch and storing it in a warm place for about twenty-four hours, or until thickened. Crème fraîche should be covered and refrigerated; it will keep for about a week.

Butter: Butter is a natural product with a wonderful flavor that I prefer to that of margarine or vegetable shortening, products I don't use.

For most cakes, it is important to cream room temperature butter with the sugar very thoroughly to incorporate air into the cake batter. When making cookies, however, cream the butter only enough to mix it thoroughly with the sugar. Overbeating the butter will cause cookies to spread.

The recipes in this book all call for unsalted butter. Salted butter contains about ¼ teaspoon of salt per stick; if you use salted butter, adjust any salt in the recipe accordingly.

Flour: Either bleached or unbleached flour is suitable for the recipes in this book, although I prefer unbleached whenever possible. Unless otherwise noted, by flour I mean all-purpose flour.

Because flour compacts under its weight measure it by spooning it into a graduated measuring cup and sweeping away the excess with the back of a knife.

Tapioca Flour: Pearls of tapioca are made by squeezing manioc root over a hot plate; when the sap hits the plate, it bounces off in little balls, or pearls. Grind pearls of tapioca into a fine powder and you get tapioca flour, an excellent thickener. It has very little flavor and is translucent when it thickens, keeping fruit pie fillings bright. To substitute tapioca flour for wheat flour as a thickener, use 25 percent less than the recipe calls for. Tapioca flour is available at Asian markets and from the King Arthur Flour Company (see Sources, page 204).

Sugar: Most home bakers will use only three types of sugar: powdered (or confectioners') sugar, granulated white sugar, and brown sugar. Powdered sugar is finely pulverized sugar with 3 percent cornstarch added to prevent caking. I use it for dusting cakes and cookies.

Granulated sugar is what is called for in recipes when the type of sugar is not specified. I prefer cane sugar, which is always labeled as such.

Brown sugar is white sugar that has been centrifuged with a molasseslike cane syrup. Since the centrifuging aerates the sugar, it needs to be packed into a measuring cup for proper measurement. Dark and light brown sugar can be interchanged in recipes, depending on the strength of flavor you want. You can mix together 1 cup of white sugar with ¼ cup of molasses to make a substitute for 1 cup of light brown sugar.

Crystal sugar and raw sugar (often called turbinado sugar) have large crystals, which, when sprinkled over a cookie or pastry before baking, give the finished dessert a pleasing crunch. Raw sugar is pale amber in color, while crystal sugar is white or translucent. Hawaiian washed raw sugar made by C & H Sugar Company is usually available in supermarkets on the West Coast. You can buy crystal sugar from Sweet Celebrations (see Sources, page 205).

Eggs: Make every attempt to use the freshest eggs possible, and don't buy them if they haven't been refrigerated.

All the recipes in this book call for large eggs. When a recipe calls for room temperature eggs, remove them from the refrigerator 30 minutes before using. If you forget to take them out, put the eggs (in their shells) in a bowl filled with warm water for 5 minutes before using.

Salmonella in raw eggs is a cause for concern. Salmonella is rarely found in egg whites, however. Oven-baked custards do not pose a hazard, but if you have health concerns, custards cooked on the stove top (for ice cream, pastry cream, and crème anglaise) should be checked with an instant-read thermometer. Health experts say salmonella cannot survive if the temperature is brought up to 160 degrees or if the eggs are held at 140 degrees for at least 5 minutes.

Nuts: When nuts are called for in a recipe, whole nuts are meant. Nuts are coarsely chopped when they have been cut into large, irregular pieces, each about one-fourth or one-third the size of the whole nut. Nuts are finely chopped when the pieces are about the size of peppercorns. Pulverized nuts are ground to a very fine powder, often in a food processor or with a mechanical nut grinder.

The primary enemy of nuts is rancidity. Pecans and hazelnuts are especially vulnerable. Check for visible mold or signs of infestation before buying.

Toasting enhances the flavor of nuts and makes them crisp. Nuts can be toasted on an ungreased baking sheet in a 350-degree oven for 7 to 10 minutes. When done, they'll smell nutty and the flesh will have turned a light shade of brown. Keep an eye on the nuts while they are toasting and stir them occasionally to prevent burning.

Almond paste is usually a mixture of equal parts blanched almonds and sugar, ground and kneaded into a paste. You can find it at most supermarkets and specialty food stores, sold in 7-ounce tubes, or you can mail-order it from Amoretti (see Sources, page 203), where it is made fresh weekly.

Vanilla Extract and Vanilla Beans: I use pure Bourbon vanilla extract, which has a bold vanilla flavor. If you prefer, you can use the more costly Tahitian vanilla, which has a delicate floral scent and flavor. Vanilla extract will keep 4 to 5 years if kept tightly capped.

Vanilla beans, the fragrant dried and cured pods of a tropical orchid, are ideal for steeping in ice cream and custard mixtures. Avoid cheap beans, which often smell smoky, and ones that appear to be dried out and brittle. Taking a good sniff should give you a good idea of the quality of the beans. Store vanilla beans in an airtight container in a cool, dry place—but not in the refrigerator, where the moisture is an invitation to mold.

To use vanilla beans, split them lengthwise with a paring knife and scrape the tiny flavorful seeds into whatever you're cooking. The pod can be use for infusing flavor as well. You can reuse the pods by rinsing and drying them thoroughly, then storing them imbedded in white sugar, or in a jar of rum or bourbon.

Alcohol: Any alcohol used in baking should always be of the highest quality, especially since it will most likely be consumed outside the kitchen as well, at least it will in my house. I always have on hand dark rum, Cognac, bourbon, green Chartreuse, kirsch, pear eau-de-vie, and Grand Marnier. A wonderful source for excellent kirsch and other fruit distillations is St. George Spirits (see Sources, page 205).

Gelatin: To use gelatin, sprinkle it over the surface of cold water and allow it to soften undisturbed for 5 minutes. To melt it, stir it over very low heat until just dissolved or pour hot liquid over it. Gelatin begins to firm up quickly as it chills, and will continue to set for the next 24 to 36 hours. If you want a gelatin dessert to set quickly, stir it in a metal bowl set over an ice bath, stirring constantly with a rubber scraper to keep every bit of the mixture in constant motion to promote even jelling and discourage lumps from forming.

Baking Powder: Use only baking powder that is aluminum-free. A good brand is Rumford, available at natural food stores and some grocery stores. It has no bitter metallic aftertaste. Replace baking powder that is over 6 months old, or test it by mixing some with a small amount of hot water—it should bubble vigorously.

FRUITS

Fruit—plain fruit—is an incomparable dessert all by itself. And if the fruit in question is absolutely delicious as is, it would be superfluous to fool around with it much. If you bought only a few pounds of perfectly ripe, extra-sweet apricots with their own uniquely complex, spicy flavor, it would be absurd to use them all up in, say, a triple mousse cake, in which they would smother under competing flavors and excessive sweetness. Better to serve them unfussed with. Later on in this cookbook there is a whole chapter of fruit desserts—baked and stuffed; in puddings and compotes; in pies, tarts, and galettes—but they are only at their best when they are featuring fresh fruit that's utterly ripe and exquisitely flavorful.

When people ask me how you tell when something's ripe, they often sound as if they think there must be some mysterious secret I know and they don't. But there isn't, really. Knowing where and when to smell out the best fruit, and how to choose it, and knowing when it's ripe is knowledge you have to experience as much as learn from books. But here are a few broad hints: Use your nose. Don't be afraid to try something new. And the closer you can get to the source, the more you'll learn.

Trips to farmer's markets and roadside stands can yield unexpected surprises: scarce sour cherries, white doughnut-shaped peaches—or a hand-crafted locally produced cheese to serve with Comice pear slices and toasted walnuts for a perfectly simple dessert.

Apples: Apples are a dependable fruit, readily available and inexpensive. Interestingly enough, varieties that are wonderful eaten raw sometimes lose their flavor when baked.

In California, our season begins in August with the sudden appearance of Gravenstein apples from Sonoma County. A classic cooking apple, Gravensteins are intensely flavorful when cooked. Buy only ripe Gravenstein apples with vivid red stripes; the green ones have been rushed to market underripe. Gravensteins must be kept refrigerated.

Common apple varieties for baking that are widely available include Golden Delicious, Granny Smith, McIntosh, Red Delicious, Baldwin, Pippin, Rome Beauty, Cortland, and Jonathan. Golden Delicious apples are good for both baking and eating, and dependably hold their shape when cooked. McIntoshes are very tasty cooked, although often mushy when baked. The Granny Smith, a staple in many supermarkets, is usually picked green and underripe—look for Granny Smiths that are red or yellow. Other good varieties for cooking are Stayman Winesap, Northern Spy, Pippin, Sierra Beauty, and Empire. Due to a renewed interest in heirloom varieties, colorful and exotic apples such as Pink Pearl, Swaar, and Banana have begun to turn up at farmer's markets. I encourage you to seek them out and cook with them. The best apples are available in autumn and winter.

Choose apples that are firm and free of bruises. Some scarring and blemishing is normal. Store apples in the refrigerator or in a cold place until ready to use.

Apricots: Apricots are the first of the stone fruits (the ones with pits) and appear early in May, at the same time as cherries, their perfect partner. When choosing fresh apricots, look for plump orange fruits, some with a reddish cheek. Avoid those that are green. Apricots are best ripened at room temperature, in a single layer rather than piled up. When they are ripe, their flesh turns translucent and squishy soft. Ripe apricots should be refrigerated and used as soon as possible; their juiciness is an invitation to spoilage.

Familiar and delicious varieties include Casselman, Castlebrite, Perfection, and the Royal or Blenheim apricot, the best of them all.

Bananas: Because bananas have become the second most popular fruit in the United States, banana business is big business. Consequently there are only two varieties commonly available, the yellow Cavendish and the Gros Michel. I find neither variety very flavorful.

To find a truly tasty banana, look for other varieties. My favorite bananas are red ones from Mexico, less starchy and much sweeter than the commercial yellow varieties. Search for unusual bananas in Latin and Asian markets. Don't be put off by blemished exteriors. Commercial yellow bananas are heavily sprayed to ensure their perfect appearance.

Store bananas at room temperature until ripe, then use them or refrigerate until ready to use. The skin will turn black in the refrigerator but the flesh will be fine.

Berries: Our local berry season begins and ends with strawberries, which first come to market in April and disappear by November, depending on the weather. In midsummer, strawberries are joined by raspberries (red, golden, and black), boysenberries, tayberries, blueberries, huckleberries, blackberries, ollalieberries, mulberries, and currants.

Berries are always best picked ripe and eaten right away. When buying berries, be sure to check the underside of the cardboard basket. If it's damp, the berries are probably spoiled. Store berries in a single layer on a tray in the refrigerator, uncovered. When berries are plentiful, freeze them, arranging them on a platter in a single layer and putting them in the freezer. Once frozen, transfer them to freezer bags and keep in the freezer until needed.

Cherries: Cherry season is inevitably too short. The first local sweet cherries to appear in mid-May are Burlat cherries. Shortly after come Rainier, yellow Queen Ann, Tartarian, and finally meaty Bing cherries, which have the most intense flavor of all. In early July, the season is sadly over. Sour cherries, the classic pie cherries, are rarely available fresh, but occasionally appear at farmer's markets and specialty stores in late June.

Choose cherries that are plump and free of bruises with moist, perky stems, a sign that they have been picked recently. An untimely rain can cause cherries to split open as they grow. This is unattractive, but flavor is unaffected, although split cherries tend to mold rapidly. Once picked, cherries do not ripen further and should be used quickly.

Since the season is so short, I recommend candying some cherries (see page 179) or freezing pitted cherries whole.

Citrons: Citrons are prized for their aromatic musky peel, which is candied (page 167) and used as a traditional flavoring in panforte (page 160). Although candied citron is available commercially, citron you candy yourself will be better. Make sure to wash the citron thoroughly before using the rind, unless it's organically grown. The Etrog citron looks like a jumbo lemon, and the Buddha's Hand citron looks like an elongated, many-fingered hand. Citrons are best stored in the refrigerator.

Coconuts: To choose a good coconut, make sure there is no mold around the eyes and shake it to make sure there is plenty of liquid sloshing around inside. To open a fresh coconut, hold it in one hand with its eyes off to the side. With a hammer, sharply tap the coconut at its midpoint, being careful not to hit your hand. Rotate the coconut, tapping it with the hammer along its equator until it is fully cracked in two. The liquid inside is not coconut milk, as is commonly thought. Coconut milk is made by heating the liquid along with the shredded meat and steeping it for an hour, then squeezing out the milk through cheesecloth. Very good canned or frozen coconut milk from Thailand is sold inexpensively in Asian markets.

To grate fresh coconut, heat the broken coconut in a 400-degree oven for 10 to 15 minutes. Once the coconut has cooled, use a sharp vegetable peeler to shave the rough brown skin from the meat, and grate or shred the meat, either by hand or with a food processor fitted with a grating disk. One fresh coconut will yield about 3 cups of shredded coconut.

Currants: Tart red currants are used to flavor summer pudding (page 94). To use currants, rinse the clusters, then use a fork to strip the tiny berries from the stems. Red currants are in season for at most a few weeks during July and early August. Because of their intense flavor, only a few currants are needed to flavor a dessert.

Figs: Figs appear twice, during the summer and the fall. The first crop is in June and July, the second, which is generally better, in late August and September. Figs should be eaten only when very ripe; when they are extremely soft and at their bursting point, their sides sometimes split vertically as if exploding with sweetness. Black-skinned varieties to look for are the Black Mission, the most common, and the Brown Turkey, notable for its hefty size. Green-skinned figs include Kadota, Calimyrna, and the prolific Adriatic. Figs have the highest fiber content of any fruit, nut, or vegetable.

Fresh figs should be purchased as close to tree-ripe as possible. If they are firm when you buy them, arrange them in a single layer and allow them to ripen at room temperature until they are very squishy, and perhaps oozing a bit of sticky juice. Underripe figs will sometimes exude a milky liquid and will taste chalky rather than sweet and luscious.

Grapefruits: The grapefruit is a citrus hybrid, a cross between the pomelo and the orange. The sweetest varieties are Ruby Red and Marsh Ruby, both red-fleshed. A more recent hybrid, the Oro Blanco, is a re-cross of the pomelo with the grapefruit.

When not organically grown, grapefruits should be thoroughly washed if the rind is going to be used, for candied peel, for example. All citrus fruits are best stored in the refrigerator.

Kumquats: Kumquats are often included with citrus fruits, but they belong to a genus of their own. The most familiar varieties are the oval Nagami and the sweeter round Meiwa, which are both enjoyed by popping the whole fruit in your mouth, edible seeds and all. Kumquats are available from November through May and, like citrus, should be stored in the refrigerator.

Lemons: The lemons that most of us are familiar with, the Eureka and the Lisbon, are quite sour. Fragrant Meyer lemons are distinctively sweet and slightly tart at the same time. Grown primarily in California, but not yet on a commercial scale, their availability is limited.

When not organically grown, lemons should be thoroughly washed if the rind is going to be used, for candied peel, for example. Lemons are best stored in the refrigerator.

Limes: The green seedless Persian lime (often called Tahiti or Bearss) is the everyday lime. Most commercial limes are picked green and underripe, then gassed to preserve their color. I prefer to use pale yellow limes, which are sweeter and not so harshly acidic. Yellow limes are easy to mistake for lemons until they are sliced open to reveal their gentle lime-green flesh. Confusingly, Rangpur limes resemble tangerines because of their vivid orange color.

When not organically grown, limes should be thoroughly washed if the rind is going to be used, for candied peel, for example. Limes are best stored in the refrigerator.

Mangoes: Mango season begins in early spring and continues through the summer, sometimes extending well into fall. As with other fruits, the best way to choose a ripe mango is to sniff it. A ripe mango will have a pronounced sweet mango fragrance and will feel cushiony soft. In most cases, any green on the skin denotes that it has yet to fully ripen.

Hayden, Kent, and Tommy Atkins mangoes are all sweet, plump varieties with orange-yellow skin that sports a red blush. Other mangoes, like the flatter, elongated Haitian varieties, are less sweet and have a spicy character that I like. Choose whichever mangoes are ripest at the market. Slightly underripe mangoes will ripen at room temperature, but once ripe, mangoes spoil quickly and should be used right away or refrigerated.

To prepare a mango, first peel away the skin with a paring knife, exposing the bright orange flesh. Holding the mango on the counter, slice the flesh away from the large flat seed in the center, which is shaped like the whole fruit itself.

Nectarines: Nectarines are a fuzzless variety of peach, but by character they are a distinctly different fruit. Nectarines have a strong, intense flavor and are well suited to being baked (page 93). Like peaches, nectarines come in both yellow- and white-fleshed varieties: May Grand, June Glo, Fantasia, and Firebrite are good yellow-fleshed varieties. White Rose, Snow Queen, and the supersweet Arctic Queen are some of my favorite white ones. Select and ripen nectarines the same way as peaches: Buy nectarines with no signs of green and smell the stem end—it should smell sweet and fragrant. The flesh should yield to gentle pressure. Once ripe, use immediately or refrigerate until ready to use.

Nectarines are available from May through September, and are at their peak in June and August.

Oranges: Oranges are available all year, although the juiciest and sweetest are harvested in the winter months. Oranges are grown in hot, sunny climates like California, Florida, and Texas. All citrus fruits get sweeter the longer they're on the tree, but they do not get sweeter after picking. Choose unblemished fruits that feel heavy for their size, a sign they possess lots of juice. The color of the skin is not an indication of ripeness or quality, but any mold or a soft spot on the skin is a sign that the entire fruit will be off.

Sour oranges such as Sevilles are quite bitter, with thick skins and many pectin-rich seeds—perfect for jelling marmalade (see page 176).

When not organically grown, oranges, like all citrus fruits, should be thoroughly washed if the rind is going to be used, for candied peel, for example. Oranges are best stored in the refrigerator.

Passion Fruit: The passion fruits you most often come across are the strong-flavored fruit of the tropical vine *Passiflora edulis*, and resemble purple deflated eggs. Passion fruits show up in markets at all times of the year.

Choose large passion fruits, since they are often sold by the piece rather than by the pound, like kiwis. Fully ripened passion fruits have wrinkly skins. Don't buy them if there is any mold on the skin. When sliced in half, the pulp and the seeds will spill out, so it is best to hold the fruits over a bowl when opening them. Since passion fruits are costly, you will want to save every precious drop. A small amount of the juice can flavor a dessert with startling intensity.

Frozen pure passion fruit pulp is an excellent substitute for fresh; freezing doesn't affect the flavor of passion fruits. Look for them at specialty markets and well-stocked supermarkets.

Peaches: The perfect peach has been ripened on the tree. If picked unripe, they become mealy. Because they need to be treated more carefully than any other fruit, peaches are best bought at a farmer's market, since only dedicated and relatively small-scale farmers pick their peaches at their peak of ripeness and bring them to market cradled in single-layer flats to protect them.

Peach season begins in May, with the aptly named May Crest, and concludes in September, with the Carnival and the (also aptly named) Last Chance varieties. Some of my favorite varieties are Suncrest, Elegant Lady, Elberta, Flamecrest, and Cal Red. White-fleshed peaches have a higher sugar content than yellow varieties and are extremely fragile. Good varieties include Snowbrite and Babcock peaches, and the odd-looking Pintu, shaped like a flattened doughnut.

Avoid buying peaches with green on their skin; they were picked too early and won't ripen properly. The shades of red and pink on peach skins are due to varietal differences, not ripeness. Ripen peaches at room temperature in a single layer with their stem end down to prevent bruising. Check them daily. When you sniff the stem end, a ripe peach will smell very sweet and peachy. Use them immediately or refrigerate them at this point.

I always peel peaches. Whole peaches can be peeled easily: Immerse a few peaches at a time in boiling water for about 15 seconds and then plunge them into ice water. The skin will slip right off. Or make a longitudinal cut around the peach down to the pit and gently twist the halves to separate them; then remove the pit and peel the halves.

Pears: Like the apple, the pear tree is a member of the rose family, hence the dizzying fragrance of a perfectly ripened pear. To properly ripen, pears must be picked underripe, and ripened off the tree; but unlike apples, ripe pears cannot be stored for any length of time. Be careful of buying pears in late winter: Since pears ripen outward, they may be firm near the skin but rotten at the core.

Bartlett pears are usually the first to arrive at the end of summer. Ripe Bartlett pears have a russet yellow color, often with a red blush. Worth searching out are Comice and Butter pears: When perfectly ripe, they're the best eating pears. I find Anjou pears to be bland. Crisp Bosc pears are okay for eating, but they are superior to other pears for cooking and poaching since they hold their shape and cooking brings out their earthy pear flavor. Winter Nelis is another variety that is best cooked rather than eaten out of hand.

Often called apple-pears, Asian pears are, in fact, pears. Of the thirty or so varieties grown in the United States, most are quite bland and are prized chiefly for their crispness. A few are nevertheless quite tasty, so if you happen to find one you like, go back and buy more. I favor the sweet Hosui, which has a speckled, caramel-colored skin. Other flavorful varieties include the Shinko, Ya Li, and Shinseiki. Although there are varieties that have a greenish hue, most green Asian pears are underripe. Ripe ones may give slightly when squeezed, but even when ripe they are often quite firm. Don't expect much aroma—they are rarely fragrant even when sliced open. Once exposed, the flesh should look wet, a sign of ripeness. Like apples and pears, they are in season from the autumn through the early spring.

Seckel pears are tiny—some are only an inch tall—and have a distinctive floral character. They can be poached whole and served with other poached fruits in a winter compote (page 82).

When selecting pears, choose ones that are unbruised and fragrant, if possible. Ripen pears at room temperature. Pears are ripe when they yield to gentle pressure from your thumb where the stem end widens into the main body of the pear. A ripe pear will give off a sweet aroma, especially when sniffed at the flower end opposite the stem.

Persimmons: The Japanese persimmon called the Hachiya is what most people think of when imagining persimmons. Hachiya persimmons are elongated fruits with a vivid orange color. Once picked, they need to be ripened at room temperature until they are completely soft and translucent, or they will be inedibly bitter and tannic. When properly ripe, a Hachiya persimmon will look and feel like a water balloon ready to burst. If purchased rock-hard, they must ripen for at least several days, and often for a week or more. Once ripe, they can be stored in the refrigerator or freezer, either whole or puréed, until ready to use.

Persimmon season starts in October and lasts through December. To purée a ripe persimmon, pull off the stem, split the fruit in half, then scoop out the jellylike pulp. Purée in a food processor or a blender, or pass the pulp through a food mill.

The squat Fuyu persimmon is the other common persimmon, and is edible when hard. Although they can be puréed like Hachiya persimmons, they are best enjoyed peeled and sliced and eaten out of hand.

Pineapples: Contrary to popular belief, a pineapple is not ripe when the leaves pull out of the stem easily. Moreover, a pineapple does not ripen much after picking. Therefore you should choose a pineapple labeled "Jet Fresh" or "Field Fresh," which is picked ripe from the plant.

A good pineapple will smell strongly of pineapple and will have an appealing yellow color with little green on the outside (unless it is one of the few dark-green-skinned varieties). Make sure there are no rotten spots and check the stem end to be certain there is no mold. To prepare pineapple, slice or twist off the crown of leaves and slice away the stem end. Stand the pineapple on one end and slice all the skin off. Remove the eyes with the tip of a stainless steel vegetable peeler. Canned pineapple packed in its own juice makes an acceptable substitute if good fresh pineapple is not available.

Plums: Most plums grown in the United States are of Japanese origin, including the Santa Rosa, the most popular and widely available plum. Other common varieties include Laroda, Casselman, Simka, French Prune, Elephant Heart (a plum with ruby-red flesh), and Shisho and Shiro plums (these last two are yellow plums and very sweet). Kelsey plums are pretty, with green skins and yellow flesh, but their flavor is somewhat bland. The plum family also includes the smaller, late-season European varieties know as Italian or French prune plums, or when dried, simply as prunes.

Over 90 percent of the plums grown in the United States are from California, where their season lasts from May to October, peaking in July and August. Plums will ripen fine off the tree. They should be handled like other stone fruits and ripened at room temperature, in a single layer, stem ends down, until tender.

Pluots: Pluots are a relatively new apricot-plum hybrid developed in the 1980s with a higher sugar content than either apricots or plums. Their flavor is closer to a sweet plum's than to that of an apricot. Some varieties to look out for are Dapple Dandy, Flavor King, and Flavor Queen. The pluot season is short, lasting about a month in the middle of the summer. Pluots can be used in recipes in place of apricots or plums.

Quinces: A bowl of ripening quinces, one of my favorite fruits, will fill a room with a heavenly sweet fragrance. Inedible when raw, when cooked they are delicious: Their characteristic quince aroma intensifies and the flesh often turns a brilliant crimson color.

Quinces begin to appear in October and are available well into the winter. Two common varieties are Smyrna and Pineapple quinces. Buy quinces with a minimum of bruises (since they bruise easily, this may be difficult). Green quinces are underripe; leave them at room temperature until they become aromatic and yellow.

To cook quinces, rub off any woolly matter that may be on the skin. Quarter and peel them. Very carefully cut out the seeds and the cores with a paring knife. The flesh is very firm and may resist your knife, but be sure to cut away all the hard parts of the core.

Prepared quinces can be chopped or grated into a pie filling before it is baked. Or give quince slices a leisurely poaching in a sugar syrup flavored with vanilla bean and intermix the colorful slices with apple slices on the apple and frangipane galette (page 81). Because quinces are so high in pectin, they make an excellent fruit paste (page 169).

Rhubarb: Rhubarb is not a fruit, but edible leaf stalks, like celery. It is very acidic, however, so it is used as an early springtime fruit substitute, a welcome relief after a long winter of apple and pear desserts.

The earliest rhubarb is hothouse rhubarb, which has a less intense rosy color and more subdued flavor than field-grown rhubarb. Although cultivated mostly from April until the end of summer, hothouse rhubarb may appear sporadically throughout the year. Rhubarb stalks need to be carefully washed to remove any grit. Submerge the stalks in a sink or basin full of water, dry them with a towel, and trim off both ends of the stalks.

Tangerines: Tangerines and mandarines are citrus fruits with brighter, spicier flavors than oranges. Good choices for juicing include the varieties Honey, Fairchild, Dancy, and Page. Tangerine juice makes an exceptional sorbet (page 107).

When not organically grown, tangerines should be thoroughly washed if the rind is going to be used, for candied peel, for example. Tangerines are best stored in the refrigerator.

This chapter offers recipes for moist and intriguingly delicious cakes. Most of them are simple one-layer cakes that do not have to be split, multiply frosted, assembled, and decorated. Think instead of moist wedges of intense flavor served with juicy fruit compotes, or of squares of almost indecently rich chocolate cake, dusted with powdered sugar and served with a cloud of whipped cream or an unrestrained pour of crème anglaise.

For the home baker who wants to compose a layered extravaganza, I've included a three-layer coconut cake, my version of the nutty meringue cake known as marjolaine, and recipes for two chilled desserts of the trifle type, a tropical tiramisù and a Meyer lemon semifreddo, in both of which syrup-soaked sponge cake alternates in layers with a rich custard.

CAKES

COCONUT CAKE

ONE 9-INCH CAKE; 10 TO 12 SERVINGS

This is my recipe for the cake that I made every year for Alice Waters's father on his birthday. A week before that date, Alice would sidle up to me and ask, ever so politely, if I could possibly make this cake for him. I always obliged, of course: For one thing, I share his affection for this cake. It hasn't happened yet, but I wish someone would surprise me with one for my birthday.

This cake should be assembled the day before you plan to serve it, so the flavors have time to meld. It will also be much easier to slice.

1 (9-inch) round sponge cake (page 188)

The coconut custard:

2 tablespoons cornstarch

¼ cup plus 1¼ cups milk

½ cup sugar

½ vanilla bean, split

5 egg yolks

1 cup unsweetened dried coconut

The rum syrup:

2/3 cup water

½ cup sugar

3 tablespoons dark rum

The whipped cream:

1¼ cups heavy cream

1½ tablespoons sugar

¼ teaspoon vanilla extract

1¼ cups unsweetened dried coconut, toasted

1   To make the coconut custard: Stir together the cornstarch and ¼ cup of the milk with a fork until the cornstarch has dissolved.

2   Measure the 1¼ cups of milk and the sugar into a heavy saucepan. Scrape the seeds from the vanilla bean into the milk, add the vanilla pod, and warm over medium heat.

3   In a separate bowl, whisk together the egg yolks; set aside. When the milk is hot, whisk in the slurry of cornstarch and continue to cook over medium heat, stirring constantly, until the mixture thickens.

4   Whisk some of the thickened milk into the egg yolks, then add them to the rest of the mixture in the saucepan.

5   Cook, stirring constantly and scraping the bottom, until the mixture just begins to boil and becomes very thick. Do not overcook. Remove from the heat and strain into a clean bowl. Remove the vanilla pod, stir in the coconut, and cool completely. Refrigerate until ready to use.

6   To make the rum syrup: Heat the water and sugar in a saucepan until the sugar has dissolved. Remove from heat and add the rum.

7   To assemble the cake: With a long serrated knife, slice the sponge cake horizontally into three equal layers.

8   Place a layer of sponge cake on a plate. Use a pastry brush to soak the cake with 1/3 cup of the rum syrup.

9   Evenly spread half the coconut custard filling, about 1/2 cup, on top of the sponge cake layer. Cover it with a second layer of sponge cake.

10 Soak the top of the second layer with another 1/3 cup of rum syrup. Spread the remaining coconut custard over the soaked sponge cake layer. Place the final sponge cake layer on top and soak with the rest of the syrup. If possible, allow the cake to set in the refrigerator for 8 hours, or overnight.

11 To make the whipped cream: Before serving, whip the cream until it forms soft peaks, then whisk in the sugar and vanilla.

12 Use a metal spatula to coat the cake completely with the whipped cream. Cover the top and sides of the cake evenly with the toasted coconut by sprinkling coconut on top of the cake and pressing more around the sides with your hands.

Serving suggestion: *Serve hefty slices of this cake either by themselves or with a simple compote of tropical fruits and berries tossed in sugar and dark rum.*

CHOCOLATE ORBIT CAKE

ONE 9-INCH CAKE; 12 TO 14 SERVINGS

Someone told me once that this cake reminded her of the lunar surface, and somebody else added that it launches chocolate lovers into orbit.

½ **pound (2 sticks) butter**
12 ounces bittersweet chocolate
6 eggs

1 cup sugar
Optional: Crème anglaise (page 190)

1   Position the oven rack in the center of the oven. Preheat the oven to 350 degrees. Butter a 9 by 2-inch round cake pan, and line the inside with a round of parchment paper.

2   Set a large bowl over a pan of simmering water to create a double boiler. Cut the butter and chocolate into small pieces and put them in the bowl to melt, whisking occasionally.

3   Whisk together the eggs and sugar in another bowl. Thoroughly whisk in the melted chocolate.

4   Pour the chocolate batter into the cake pan. Place it in a larger baking pan, and pour in warm water to reach halfway up the sides of the cake pan. Cover tightly with foil and bake for 1 hour and 15 minutes, until the cake appears to have set and when you touch the center, your finger comes away clean.

5   Remove the cake from the water bath and cool completely before serving, plain or with crème anglaise.

Note: This cake can be refrigerated for several days.

CHOCOLATE PAVÉ

*Chocolate pavé has become
the most popular chocolate
dessert at the café at Chez
Panisse. This is an adaptation
of Lindsey Shere's recipe. It
makes a neat square of dense
chocolate cake—one of the
few desserts that is served
both upstairs in the café and
downstairs in the restaurant
dining room, to the delight of
all. Pavé means "paving stone"
in French, so in order for the
cake to be truly worthy of its
name, it must be baked in a
square cake pan or a
rectangular baking dish and
cut into pieces resembling
square-shaped pavers.*

4 ounces bittersweet chocolate

4 ounces unsweetened chocolate

½ pound (2 sticks) butter

6 eggs, separated, at room temperature

½ cup plus ½ cup sugar

Optional: Pinch of cream of tartar

Powdered sugar for dusting the cake

Optional: Melted chocolate for decorating the cake

Whipped cream (page 192) or crème anglaise (page 190)

1   Position the oven rack in the center of the oven. Preheat the oven to 350 degrees. Butter an 8 by 8 by 2-inch square cake pan or a 9 by 2-inch round cake pan and add a bit of flour or cocoa powder. Swirl the pan to evenly coat the bottom and sides with flour or cocoa and tap out the excess. Line the bottom of the pan with parchment paper.

2   Set a bowl over a pan of simmering water. Roughly chop the bittersweet chocolate and the unsweetened chocolate and melt in the bowl along with the butter, cut into small pieces. Stir occasionally until the chocolate and butter have melted smoothly together, then remove the bowl from the heat.

3   Whip the egg yolks with ½ cup of the sugar, 3 to 5 minutes in a standing electric mixer, until they lighten and form a ribbon when you lift the beater. Stir in the melted chocolate and butter until fully incorporated.

4   In a large mixing bowl, begin whisking the egg whites slowly until they are frothy. If you are not using a copper bowl, add the cream of tartar. Increase your speed and keep whisking until the egg whites form soft, wet peaks. Gradually beat in the remaining ½ cup of sugar, and continue whisking until the whites form wet, shiny peaks that hold their shape.

5   Fold the egg whites into the chocolate mixture just until there are no visible streaks of egg white. Do not overfold.

6   Transfer the batter to the prepared cake pan and gently smooth the top. Bake for 35 minutes. The cake will rise as it is baking and form a firm, slightly crackly top. To test for doneness, gently touch the center of the cake. It should still feel slightly jiggly but just barely set in the center. Remove the cake from the oven and cool about 15 minutes.

7   Turn the cake out upside down onto a baking sheet, remove the parchment paper, invert onto a serving plate, and dust the top of the cake with powdered sugar. If desired, decorate the top of the cake with melted chocolate: Dip a fork in melted chocolate and wave it back and forth a few inches over the cake, creating an abstract scribble of chocolate on the top. Serve with whipped cream or crème anglaise.

MARJOLAINE

ONE 12-INCH RECTANGULAR CAKE; 14 TO 16 SERVINGS

This is my modernized version of the cake made famous by the legendary Fernand Point at his restaurant La Pyramide, in Vienne, France. The marjolaine—layers of flavored creams sandwiched between nut meringues—was his signature dessert. It has become a classic.

This version is layered with crème fraîche, which adds a distinctive tangy flavor that contrasts pleasantly with the layers of nutty meringue. Marjolaine should be made at least a day before it is served to give the flavors a chance to mellow together.

The nut meringue:
3/4 cup hazelnuts, toasted

3/4 cup whole almonds, toasted

1 1/3 cups sugar

1 tablespoon cornstarch

8 egg whites, at room temperature

Optional: Pinch of cream of tartar

Pinch of salt

The praline:
1/2 cup whole almonds, toasted

1/2 cup sugar

The chocolate ganache:
10 ounces bittersweet chocolate, chopped

3/4 cup crème fraîche (page 8)

The vanilla and praline creams:
3/4 cup crème fraîche

1/4 cup heavy cream

2 tablespoons sugar

1/2 teaspoon vanilla extract

1 tablespoon Cognac or brandy

Whipped cream (page 192)

1   To make the nut meringue: Position the oven rack in the center of the oven and preheat the oven to 350 degrees. Butter the bottom and sides of a 12 by 18-inch baking pan. Fit a sheet of parchment paper into the bottom of the pan. Generously butter the parchment and dust the inside of the pan with flour. Tap out any excess.

2   Rub the hazelnuts between your hands to loosen and remove as much skin as possible. In a food processor, pulverize the almonds and hazelnuts with the sugar and cornstarch.

3   In a large mixing bowl, preferably copper, whisk the egg whites until they become frothy. If you are not using a copper bowl, add the optional cream of tartar to the egg whites.

4   Add the pinch of salt and increase your whisking speed, beating until the egg whites form soft, glossy peaks that droop slightly when you lift the whisk.

5   Sprinkle the ground nut mixture over the egg whites and fold the nuts into the egg whites.

6   Evenly smooth the nut meringue onto the prepared baking sheet with a spatula. Bake for 20 to 25 minutes, until pale golden brown. Cool.

7   To make the praline: See the caramelization guidelines on page 200. Lightly oil a baking sheet. Coarsely chop the almonds.

8   Sprinkle the sugar into a heavy sauté pan in an even layer. Melt the sugar over low heat, tilting the pan or gently stirring so the sugar will melt evenly. Continue cooking until the sugar turns a light amber color and caramelizes. Remove from the heat and immediately stir in the nuts with a wooden spoon. Pour the mixture onto the oiled baking sheet in an even layer and allow to cool completely at room temperature.

9   When cool, break up the praline with your hands, and finely chop it in a food processor or with a large chef's knife.

10   To make the ganache: Coarsely chop the chocolate. Heat the crème fraîche in a saucepan until it just begins to boil. Remove from the heat and add the chocolate, stirring until it's completely melted. Set aside to cool and thicken at room temperature.

11   To make the vanilla and praline creams: Whip together the crème fraîche, cream, sugar, and vanilla until the mixture becomes glossy and begins to hold its shape. Continue beating until it stiffens, but do not overbeat it.

12   Add ⅔ cup of the whipped crème fraîche mixture to the chopped praline and stir it together. It will seem somewhat stiff, but the caramel from the praline will dissolve as it stands, making the praline cream easy to spread.

13   Add the Cognac or brandy to the rest of the crème fraîche mixture, and whisk it slightly, if necessary, to firm it up.

14   With a serrated knife, cut around the edges of the meringue to release it from the pan. Place another sheet pan over it, baking side up (or use a cutting board), and invert the meringue. Carefully peel away the parchment paper, holding down the meringue as you peel it so as not to break the meringue. (If you do break the meringue, it can be patched together when you are assembling the layers.)

15   To assemble the marjolaine, cut the meringue into four rectangles, each about 4 by 12 inches.

16   Cover a baking sheet with a piece of plastic wrap. Lay down one rectangle of the meringue. With an offset spatula, evenly spread ¾ cup of the cooled chocolate ganache over it. Cover and refrigerate the remaining ganache.

17   Add the second piece of meringue, and evenly spread all the Cognac cream over it. Cover that with the third piece of meringue.

18   Evenly spread all the praline cream over the meringue, and cover it with the final piece of meringue.

19   Wrap the marjolaine in plastic wrap and refrigerate it overnight.

20   Before serving, remove the marjolaine and the ganache from the refrigerator. Trim the rough edges of the marjolaine with a long serrated knife. Gently rewarm the ganache to a spreadable consistency, over warm water, and spread it smoothly over the top and sides of the cake. To serve, slice the marjolaine into beautiful even slices, using a long serrated knife that has been dipped in hot water before each cut. Serve it with lightly whipped cream.

Note: Marjolaine will keep for several days in the refrigerator.

GÂTEAU VICTOIRE

I never understood why something without flour should be prized above something with it, but for a while the public seemed to prefer flourless chocolate cakes.

Because it requires gentle, even baking, it must be baked in a water bath. You'll need a pan for your water bath that is several inches larger than the springform pan you use. And because its flavor is the superb essence of chocolate, resist serving it with anything but sweetened whipped cream.

Gâteau victoire is extraordinary when made with Scharffen Berger chocolate (see Sources, page 205).

Note: Since this cake is quite delicate, it can be sliced most easily by holding a sufficient length of dental floss taut between your two hands and pushing it straight down through the cake, cutting it into two half circles. Remove the floss by letting go of one end and pulling the other out the side, not by pulling back up. Make successive cuts in the same way.

2 teaspoons cocoa	6 eggs, at room temperature
12 ounces bittersweet chocolate	6 tablespoons sugar
3/4 cup heavy cream	Powdered sugar for dusting the cake
3 tablespoons dark rum or Cognac	Whipped cream (page 192)

1   Position the oven rack in the center of the oven. Preheat the oven to 350 degrees. Liberally butter a 9½-inch springform pan. Cut a circle of parchment paper to fit inside the bottom of the pan. Place the parchment in the pan and smooth it against the bottom. Brush the parchment circle with butter. Dust the pan with 2 teaspoons of cocoa and tap out the excess.

2   Coarsely chop the chocolate. In a large mixing bowl, combine the chocolate, the heavy cream, and the rum or Cognac. Set the bowl over a pan of simmering water to melt the chocolate, stirring occasionally. When the chocolate has melted, remove the bowl from the heat.

3   In an electric mixer, using the whisk attachment, beat the eggs and the sugar for about 5 minutes, until they form a well-defined ribbon.

4   Fold one third of the beaten egg mixture into the melted chocolate and cream to lighten it. Then fold in the rest. Transfer the batter to the prepared pan. Set the cake pan inside a deep ovenproof pan, and add hot water until it reaches halfway up the side of the cake pan.

5   Bake for 45 minutes, or until the cake feels just set in the center. Remove from the oven, wait a few minutes, then remove the cake from the water bath. Cool completely.

6   Run a knife along the edges of the cake to loosen it from the sides of the pan. Release the sides of the springform pan and remove any pieces of crust that may have come loose. Invert the cake onto a serving plate and carefully remove the bottom of the springform pan and the parchment paper. Dust with powdered sugar and serve with whipped cream.

CHOCOLATE MACADAMIA CAKE

ONE 9½-INCH ROUND CAKE; 10 TO 12 SERVINGS

This recipe has only four ingredients, it can be assembled in minutes, and it produces a cake so intensely chocolate-flavored that the only thing you will want to serve alongside it will be softly whipped cream. Use the very best chocolate you can find. If you want, substitute walnuts or pistachios for the macadamias—or leave out nuts altogether.

¾ **pound (3 sticks) unsalted butter**

1½ **pounds bittersweet chocolate (see Note)**

1 **cup macadamia nuts, toasted**

8 **eggs, at room temperature**

Whipped cream (page 192)

1   Position the oven rack in the center of the oven. Preheat the oven to 400 degrees. Butter a 9½-inch springform cake pan and line the bottom with a round of parchment paper.

2   Cut the butter into small pieces and chop the chocolate into small pieces. In a large bowl set over hot water, melt the chocolate and butter together. Coarsely chop the macadamia nuts.

3   With an electric mixer, beat the eggs until a ribbon forms when you lift the beater.

4   Fold the eggs into the melted butter and chocolate, and then rapidly fold in the nuts.

5   Transfer the batter to the lined springform pan and bake in the preheated oven for 45 minutes. If the cake appears to be getting too dark on top, drape a piece of aluminum foil over it and continue baking until the cake begins to feel firm in the center.

6   When the cake has cooled, loosen the cake by running a knife around the sides of the pan and remove the sides of the springform pan. Invert the cake onto a serving plate, lift off the botttom of the springform pan and peel away the parchment paper. Turn the cake onto a serving plate. Serve with whipped cream.

Note: Because this cake has no added sugar, I recommend using a chocolate that is not overly bitter.

PISTACHIO AND CARDAMOM CAKE WITH APRICOTS POACHED IN SAUTERNES

ONE 9-INCH CAKE; 10 TO 12 SERVINGS

An unusual cake with an almond-sugar crust, aggressively spiced with cardamom, to me the most sophisticated of spices— complex, smoky, aromatic, and elusive. Once I start eating anything with cardamom I can't stop. A worthwhile variation is to add freshly grated orange zest to the batter. The apricots poached in Sauternes are so good with this cake that I include them as part of the recipe, even though they technically belong with the other poached fruit recipes.

The apricots:

1 cup water

½ cup sugar

¼ vanilla bean, split

½ cup Sauternes or similar dessert wine

4 fresh ripe apricots, or ½ pound dried apricots

The almond topping:

2 tablespoons butter

1 teaspoon sugar

¾ cup sliced almonds (preferably unblanched)

The pistachio and cardamom cake:

¾ cup shelled pistachios

¾ cup plus ¼ cup flour

8 tablespoons (1 stick) butter, at room temperature

1 cup sugar

3 eggs, at room temperature

1 teaspoon baking powder

Pinch of salt

2 teaspoons cardamom seeds, ground

1   To poach the apricots: First bring the water and sugar to a boil in a medium-size saucepan. Add the vanilla bean and Sauternes, and reduce the heat so the syrup is at a simmer.

2   Cut the apricots in half and remove the pits. Add the apricot halves to the syrup and poach for about 10 minutes, until the apricots soften. If you use dried apricots, poach them until tender, from 30 to 45 minutes.

3   Remove from the heat and let stand until the cake is almost ready to serve. Or you can poach the apricots several days in advance. The longer they stand in the syrup, the more intense their Sauternes flavor.

4   To make the almond topping for the cake: Melt the 2 table-spoons of butter in a 9 by 2-inch cake pan. Remove from heat and cool briefly. Sprinkle the teaspoon of sugar evenly over the butter, then add the sliced almonds, tilting and shaking the pan to distribute them evenly. Set the pan aside while you make the cake batter.

5   To make the pistachio and cardamom cake: Position the oven rack in the center of the oven. Preheat the oven to 350 degrees.

6   In a food processor, pulverize the pistachios with ¼ cup of the flour, as finely as possible.

7   Beat together the butter and sugar, beating until very light and fluffy, about 5 minutes if you are using an electric mixer. If you are using a mixer, stop once or twice to scrape down the sides of the bowl.

8   Add the eggs, one at a time, beating slowly and stopping the mixer to scrape down any unincorporated batter. After the eggs have been added, the batter may look slightly curdled. This is normal.

9   Sift together the remaining ¾ cup flour, baking powder, and salt, and stir into the batter. Mix in the pistachio-flour mixture and ground cardamom seeds.

10   Transfer the batter to the prepared cake pan by making four or five mounds of batter on top of the almonds. Carefully spread the batter into an even layer, disturbing the almond-sugar topping as little as possible.

11   Bake the cake for 40 minutes, or until a toothpick inserted in the center comes out clean. Remove from the oven and let cool for 15 to 30 minutes. While the cake is cooling, remove the apricots from their liquid, and reduce the liquid by about half, until thick and syrupy.

12   Use a knife to loosen the sides of the cake from the pan. Wearing oven mitts, invert a serving plate over the cake pan, then simultaneously flip over both the plate and the cake. If necessary, shake gently or tap the upturned bottom of the cake pan to release the cake. Serve with the poached apricots and their syrup.

PERSIMMON CAKE

ONE 9- OR 9½-INCH CAKE; 10 TO 12 SERVINGS

For this dense, moist cake, I use very ripe persimmons that are completely soft and translucent. The larger, elongated Hachiya variety is best for baking, although the other common persimmon, the Fuyu, will do.

2 very ripe, medium-size persimmons

1 cup walnuts, toasted

8 tablespoons (1 stick) butter, at room temperature

1¼ cups sugar

½ teaspoon vanilla extract

2 eggs, at room temperature

1¾ cups flour

½ teaspoon salt

1 teaspoon baking soda

1 teaspoon ground cinnamon

¾ cup dried currants, soaked in ¼ cup Cognac or brandy

Powdered sugar for dusting the cake

Whipped cream (page 192)

1   Cut the persimmons in half and scoop out the pulpy flesh with a spoon. Purée the pulp in a food processor or a blender, or pass through a food mill. You will need 1 cup of the purée for the cake. (You can freeze any leftover purée and use it another time.)

2   Position the oven rack in the center of the oven and preheat the oven to 350 degrees. Line a 9-inch round cake pan or a 9½-inch springform pan with a circle of parchment paper.

3   Finely chop the walnuts.

4   Cream together the butter and sugar until light and fluffy, 3 to 5 minutes in a standing electric mixer. Add the vanilla and beat in the eggs, one at a time. Stop and scrape down the sides of the bowl and beat until the eggs are completely incorporated.

5   Sift together the flour, salt, baking soda, and cinnamon.

6   Stir half the persimmon purée into the creamed butter mixture, then thoroughly mix in the dry ingredients. Stir in the remaining purée and the walnuts, and currants with their liquor. Pour the batter into the prepared cake pan and bake about 45 minutes, until a toothpick inserted in the center comes out clean. Remove from the oven and cool.

7   Remove the cake from the pan and peel off the parchment paper. Dust with powdered sugar, and serve with whipped cream.

PLUM HUCKLEBERRY UPSIDE-DOWN CAKE

ONE 9-INCH ROUND CAKE OR 10-INCH SQUARE CAKE;
10 TO 12 SERVINGS

Upside-down cake is best enjoyed still warm from the oven. This one's my favorite, with its brown sugar topping baked together with tart plums and huckleberries. When I can't get huckleberries, I use blueberries: The wild ones are best. Sometimes some of the caramelized topping sticks to the inside of the pan when you lift it off the cake. You can scrape it out of the pan and place it back onto the cake; I just eat it, though.

The plum huckleberry topping:

3 tablespoons butter

¾ cup light brown sugar, firmly packed

1 cup (4 ounces) huckleberries

6 to 8 medium plums (about 1 pound)

The cake:

8 tablespoons (1 stick) butter, at room temperature

¾ cup sugar

1 teaspoon vanilla extract

2 eggs

1½ cups flour

1½ teaspoons baking powder

¼ teaspoon salt

½ cup milk, at room temperature

Whipped cream (page 192) or vanilla ice cream (page 121)

1   To make the plum huckleberry topping: Melt the butter in a 9-inch round cake pan or a 10-inch square cake pan, directly on the stove top, over low heat. Add the brown sugar and stir until the sugar is thoroughly moistened. Remove from the heat and cool briefly.

2   Sprinkle half of the huckleberries evenly over the moistened brown sugar. Cut the plums in half, remove the pits, and cut the plum halves into ½-inch slices. Arrange the plum slices over the huckleberries in concentric, overlapping circles, or just scatter them evenly. Strew the rest of the huckleberries on top of the plum slices.

3   To make the cake: Position the oven rack in the center of the oven and preheat the oven to 350 degrees.

4   Beat together the butter and sugar until light and fluffy, 3 to 5 minutes in a standing electric mixer. Stop the mixer once and scrape down the sides of the bowl to make sure the butter is completely incorporated. Add the vanilla.

5   Beat in the eggs, one at a time, until completely incorporated.

6   In a separate bowl, sift together the flour, baking powder, and salt. Mix half of the flour mixture into the batter. Stir the milk into the batter, add the remaining dry ingredients, and stir just until smooth; do not overmix. The batter will be quite thick.

7   Carefully spread the batter over the fruit in the cake pan, smoothing with a spatula. Bake the upside-down cake for about 1 hour, until the top is golden brown and a toothpick inserted in the center comes out clean.

8   Let the cake stand at least 20 minutes before unmolding. Run a knife around the edge of the cake to loosen it from the pan. Invert a serving plate over the cake and carefully flip over both cake and plate simultaneously. Lift off the cake pan and scrape any fruit that may have stuck to the pan back onto the cake—or enjoy it yourself. Serve with whipped cream or vanilla ice cream.

Variation: *Make the topping with 6 medium apricots instead of plums, and substitute 1 cup of any kind of berries (except strawberries) for the huckleberries.*

MEYER LEMON SEMIFREDDO

8 SERVINGS

This is my version of a semifreddo my colleague Linda Zagula made one morning at Chez Panisse. There were a few Meyer lemons on the counter, probably from a neighbor's backyard, and there was a little bit of leftover lemon curd in the refrigerator. Linda was inspired to produce gigantic quantities of a spectacular dessert from rather modest beginnings.

This is a dessert for lemon lovers. It's light but supersaturated with lemon flavor. You can substitute store-bought Amaretti di Saronno for homemade amaretti, but if you use tart Eureka lemons instead of Meyer lemons, add ¼ cup more sugar to both the lemon syrup and the lemon curd. The semifreddo's several components—sponge cake, lemon syrup, lemon curd, and amaretti—can all be made in advance and the dessert assembled at your leisure.

The Meyer lemon curd:
½ cup Meyer lemon juice (about 3 lemons)

⅓ cup sugar

6 tablespoons (¾ stick) butter, cut into pieces

2 eggs

2 egg yolks

The Meyer lemon syrup:
¾ cup water

¼ cup sugar

¼ cup Meyer lemon juice

Optional: 2 tablespoons kirsch

The assembly:
1 rectangular sponge cake (page 188)

1 cup heavy cream

¾ cup crushed amaretti cookies (about 25 cookies) (page 157)

Raspberry or blackberry sauce (page 198)

1   To make the lemon curd: Measure the lemon juice, sugar, and butter into a nonreactive saucepan, and set over low heat.

2   Briefly whisk together the eggs and egg yolks in a bowl.

3   When the butter has melted, whisk some of the warm liquid from the saucepan into the egg mixture, then stir the warmed eggs back into the liquid in the saucepan. Stir constantly with a wooden paddle or a heatproof spatula until the curd starts thickening and looks slightly jelled.

4   Press the lemon curd through a strainer into a container. Cover and refrigerate until ready to use. (The lemon curd can be made up to a week in advance.)

5   To make the lemon syrup: Heat the water and sugar together until the sugar has dissolved. Remove from the heat, and stir in the Meyer lemon juice and the kirsch, if using.

6   To assemble the semifreddo: Remove the parchment paper and cut the sponge cake into two pieces that will fit a 2-quart baking dish or soufflé mold. (You will have extra sponge cake left over that can be frozen for future use.)

7   Whip the cream until it forms soft peaks. Fold together the whipped cream and the chilled lemon curd.

8   Spread 1 cup of the lemon-cream mixture evenly in the bottom of the baking dish. Place one of the pieces of sponge cake on top of the lemon cream. With a pastry brush, soak the sponge cake with about ½ cup of the lemon syrup.

9   Spread 1 more cup of the lemon cream evenly on top of the first sponge cake layer, and sprinkle with ½ cup of the amaretti crumbs. Lay the second piece of sponge cake on top and soak it with the rest of the syrup.

10   Top with the remaining lemon cream spread in an even layer. Refrigerate, uncovered, for 30 minutes, then cover with plastic wrap, and refrigerate until ready to serve—preferably overnight, to give the semifreddo time to mellow. Before serving, sprinkle the remaining amaretti crumbs over the top. Serve the semifreddo with raspberry or blackberry sauce, or with berries tossed in sugar.

MAPLE WALNUT–PEAR CAKE

ONE 9-INCH CAKE; 10 TO 12 SERVINGS

A little while ago, I received a whole gallon of Grade B maple syrup from some friends in upstate New York. What a gift! This is one of the desserts I invented to help use up my sweet windfall.

Dark maple syrup—Grade B or Grade A "dark amber"—has a more intense maple flavor, which I prefer.

The glazed pear topping:

¼ cup dark or light brown sugar, firmly packed

⅓ cup maple syrup

½ cup walnuts, toasted

3 ripe Bosc pears

The cake batter:

8 tablespoons (1 stick) butter, at room temperature

½ cup granulated sugar

¼ cup light brown sugar firmly packed

½ teaspoon vanilla extract

2 eggs, at room temperature

1½ cups flour

1 teaspoon baking powder

2 teaspoons ground cinnamon

½ teaspoon salt

½ cup milk, at room temperature

Whipped cream (page 192)

1   Position the oven rack in the center of the oven and preheat the oven to 350 degrees.

2   To make the glazed pear topping: Combine the brown sugar and maple syrup in a 9 by 2-inch round cake pan. Set the pan directly on the stove top and heat until the mixture begins to bubble. Boil gently for 1 minute, stirring frequently. Remove the pan from the heat and set aside.

3   Coarsely chop the walnuts and sprinkle them evenly over the maple glaze in the cake pan. Press them lightly into the glaze. Quarter the pears, then peel and core them carefully, removing not just the seeds, but all the fibrous parts. Cut the quarters into ¼-inch slices, lengthwise. Arrange the pear slices concentrically, overlapping each other, making a circular pattern over the walnuts.

4   To make the cake batter: Beat together the butter, granulated sugar, and brown sugar. If you are using an electric mixer, stop it once and scrape down the sides of the bowl. Continue beating until the mixture is completely smooth and no lumps of butter are visible.

5   Add the vanilla extract and the eggs, one at a time. Stop and scrape down the sides of the bowl, then beat until the eggs are completely incorporated.

6   Sift together the flour, baking powder, cinnamon, and salt into a separate bowl. Gradually mix half the dry ingredients into the butter mixture. Stir in the milk, then add the rest of the dry ingredients, and mix until just combined.

7   Transfer the batter to the cake pan on top of the pears. Smooth it into an even layer, being careful not to disturb the arrangement of the pears.

8   Bake about 50 minutes, until a toothpick inserted into the center comes out clean. Let cool for 30 minutes. Invert a serving plate over the pan, grasp both the pan and the plate, and turn over. Lift off the cake pan. Any walnuts that may have stuck to the pan can be loosened with a fork and reunited with the cake. Serve warm, with whipped cream.

FRESH GINGER CAKE

ONE 9- OR 9½-INCH CAKE; 10 TO 12 SERVINGS

This is the most often requested recipe in my repertoire, and I've passed it on to many, many people. It appears so often on Bay Area menus (sometimes called Dave's ginger cake, which, I admit, amuses and flatters me) that I sometimes think I'm responsible for too much of a good thing. Then I order it, taste it, and decide not to worry: This simple cake is wonderful.

It stays moist for days. My favorite accompaniment for ginger cake will always be the compote of plums and raspberries on page 96, but I also like this cake served with sliced, sugared peaches or nectarines in the summer, and in the winter with a dollop of tart lemon curd (page 40) lightened a little with whipped cream.

4 ounces fresh ginger
1 cup mild molasses
1 cup sugar
1 cup vegetable oil, preferably peanut
2½ cups flour
1 teaspoon ground cinnamon
½ teaspoon ground cloves
½ teaspoon ground black pepper
1 cup water
2 teaspoons baking soda
2 eggs, at room temperature

1   Position the oven rack in the center of the oven. Preheat the oven to 350 degrees. Line a 9 by 3-inch round cake pan or a 9½-inch springform pan with a circle of parchment paper.

2   Peel, slice, and chop the ginger very fine with a knife (or use a grater).

3   Mix together the molasses, sugar, and oil. In another bowl, sift together the flour, cinnamon, cloves, and black pepper.

4   Bring the water to the boil in a saucepan, stir in the baking soda, and then mix the hot water into the molasses mixture. Stir in the ginger.

5   Gradually whisk the dry ingredients into the batter. Add the eggs, and continue mixing until everything is thoroughly combined. Pour the batter into the prepared cake pan and bake for about 1 hour, until the top of the cake springs back lightly when pressed or a toothpick inserted into the center comes out clean. If the top of the cake browns too quickly before the cake is done, drape a piece of foil over it and continue baking.

6   Cool the cake for at least 30 minutes. Run a knife around the edge of the cake to loosen it from the pan. Remove the cake from the pan and peel off the parchment paper.

TROPICAL TIRAMISÙ

8 SERVINGS

This recipe is not a real tiramisù, but it is assembled just like the Italian classic, in layers of custard and liquor-soaked sponge cake—in this case, soaked in a syrup of dark rum, sugar, and lime juice.

Making a tropical tiramisù is a process of several steps, but the final assembly takes only minutes. The sponge cake can be baked a few days in advance, and the custard can be made the day before the final assembly. When it's time to assemble the dessert, all you need to prepare is the fruit filling. Then let the assembled tiramisù sit in the refrigerator for a day before you serve it, to give the flavors a chance to meld together.

Whenever I make this at home, we sit around with spoons eating it communally, right out of the serving bowl— for some reason, that's the most fun way to eat this dessert.

The coconut custard:

½ cup sugar

1¼ cups whole milk

½ vanilla bean, split

3 tablespoons cornstarch

½ cup canned Thai coconut milk

4 egg yolks

1 cup unsweetened dried coconut

The fruit filling:

1 pineapple, peeled, cored, eyes removed, and cut into 1-inch pieces

1 pint basket strawberries, washed, hulled, and sliced

1 medium mango, peeled and cut into ½-inch cubes

6 tablespoons sugar

Juice of ½ lime

½ cup dark rum

The assembly:

1 rectangular sponge cake (page 188)

1   To make the coconut custard: Heat the sugar and whole milk together in a saucepan over medium heat. Scrape the seeds from the vanilla bean into the milk, then add the scraped bean.

2   Whisk together the cornstarch and coconut milk until completely smooth and free of lumps.

3   When the milk and sugar mixture is hot, whisk in the coconut milk mixture and continue cooking, stirring continuously, until the mixture becomes very thick.

4   Stir the egg yolks together in a bowl. Pour some of the warm thickened milk into the egg yolks, stirring constantly. Then pour the warmed egg yolks back into the saucepan with the rest of the thickened milk.

5   Keep cooking and stirring until the custard becomes quite thick, but do not overcook. Remove from the heat and scrape into a clean bowl. Remove the vanilla bean, and stir in the coconut. Refrigerate the custard, stirring it every so often while it chills to help it cool faster.

6   To make the fruit filling: Gently heat the pineapple in a sauté pan until it is lightly cooked through, 3 to 5 minutes. Cool completely.

7   Toss together the strawberries, pineapple, and mango with the sugar, lime juice, and rum.

8   To assemble the tiramisù: Use a 2-quart soufflé dish that is 3½ inches deep and 8 inches in diameter (or any glass or porcelain casserole dish that's about the same size). Remove the parchment paper from the sponge cake and cut out two pieces that will fit the dish you are using, reserving the trimmings for the middle layer. Evenly spread ½ cup of the coconut custard in the bottom of the dish. Cover the custard with a piece of sponge cake. Spread half of the fruit and its juices, about 1½ cups, over the cake.

9   Spread about 1 cup of the coconut custard over the fruit, then make another layer of sponge cake using the cut-up trimmings. Cover it with the rest of the fruit. Spread another cup of the coconut custard over the fruit, and cover with the remaining round of cake.

10   Spread the rest of the coconut custard over the top and refrigerate uncovered for about 30 minutes. Once the top layer of custard has chilled, cover with plastic wrap, and refrigerate until serving, preferably overnight. (If covered too soon, the custard sticks to the plastic.) To serve, scoop out big spoonfuls of the tiramisù so all the layers of fruit, cake, and custard can be seen.

Variations: *Depending on what fruit is available, I often add other tropical fruits, such as passion fruit pulp and papaya, and other kinds of berries. This dessert also looks and tastes great with freshly grated and toasted coconut strewn over the top.*

PASSION FRUIT POUND CAKE

ONE 9-INCH LOAF; 10 SERVINGS

The assertive, tangy passion fruit glaze soaking the cake ensures a moist and flavorful pound cake. If you can't find fresh passion fruits, you should be able to find frozen passion fruit pulp. Fresh orange juice is a good substitute. Be sure you don't dissolve the sugar when you mix the glaze, so the coating stays crunchy. I like this intensely flavored glaze so much, I've thought about baking the cake in a flat sheet so there would be more surface area to glaze.

The pound cake:

12 tablespoons (1½ sticks) butter, at room temperature

1 cup sugar

Grated zest of 2 oranges

1 teaspoon vanilla extract

3 eggs, at room temperature

1½ cups flour

1 teaspoon baking powder

Pinch of salt

The passion fruit glaze:

½ cup passion fruit juice (about 6 passion fruits, see Note), or ½ cup orange juice

⅓ cup sugar

1   Position the oven rack in the center of the oven and preheat the oven to 350 degrees. Butter and flour a 9-inch loaf pan.

2   To make the pound cake: Beat together the butter, sugar, and orange zest until light and fluffy, about 3 to 5 minutes in an electric mixer. Stop the mixer and scrape down the sides to make sure the butter is fully incorporated. Add the vanilla.

3   Beat in the eggs one at a time, waiting until each one is fully incorporated before adding the next.

4   Sift together the flour, baking powder, and salt into a separate bowl. Stir the dry ingredients into the butter and sugar mixture until the batter is just smooth. Transfer the batter to the loaf pan, smooth the top, and bake for about 1 hour, until a toothpick inserted into the center comes out clean. Allow the cake to cool about 15 minutes.

5   To prepare the passion fruit glaze: While the cake is cooling, briefly stir together the passion fruit juice and the sugar. You don't want the sugar to dissolve. Loosen the cake from the loaf pan by running a knife around the edge of the cake. Remove the warm cake from the pan and set it on a plate.

6   Pierce the cake repeatedly all the way through, top to bottom, with a wooden skewer or toothpick, about fifty times. Spoon half of the glaze over the top of the cake. Turn the cake and spoon the rest of the glaze over all the sides. Sop up the glaze that collects in the plate by rubbing the bottom and sides of the cake in it. Serve warm, preferably.

Note: To get the juice out of fresh passion fruits, split them in half and scoop the pulp into a sieve set over a bowl, pressing the pulp to separate the seeds from the juice.

This chapter is
dedicated to the
desserts that
represent the
glorification of the
humble egg: custards
and soufflés. Can anyone
withstand the smooth and
creamy appeal of a well–
made custard? I don't think so.
And I have yet to meet anyone
who isn't impressed by a steaming
soufflé brought to the table, toplofty and
seemingly lighter than air.

CUSTARDS AND SOUFFLÉS

It pays to be careful while baking custards; the baking times I've given are only approximations. Custards will bake faster or slower depending on the oven and on the temperature of the mixture. If it has been refrigerated, obviously it will take longer to bake. The variables matter, so watch carefully—you will soon develop a feel for the point at which custards are perfectly baked. When custards are close to being done, I often remove the pan containing the custards in their water bath from the oven, and let it stand, covered, checking every few minutes. It's impossible to overcook them this way.

As for soufflés, every evening that soufflés were on the menu at Chez Panisse was a real workout for me. Imagine making fifty soufflés in 1 hour, and then having to do it all over again an hour later for the next seating. After making thousands of them, I learned where the real challenge lies: not in making soufflés rise properly, which is easy, but in keeping my egg white–beating arm in good enough shape!

BLACK CURRANT TEA CRÈME BRÛLÉE

6 SERVINGS

Although I didn't jump on the bandwagon when crème brûlée was the dessert of the moment, I do like this one, especially when it comes out of the oven and I get a big noseful of its smoky, fruity aroma. It is ideal for ending a meal, especially an exotic one, on an unusual note. I buy tea from a local tea merchant in small quantities so that it is always fresh. Tea loses its aroma and character quickly.

Feel free to experiment with other teas, such as Earl Grey, which is scented with the citrus bergamot, or other fruit-flavored black teas.

3 cups heavy cream

6 tablespoons sugar, plus ¾ cup for caramelizing the custards

3 to 4 tablespoons black currant tea leaves

6 egg yolks

1   In a saucepan, warm together the cream, 6 tablespoons sugar, and tea leaves. Steep for 30 minutes, or until you are satisfied with the flavor.

2   Position the oven rack in the center of the oven and preheat the oven to 350 degrees.

3   Lightly whisk the egg yolks. Whisking constantly, slowly pour in the warm tea infusion. Strain into a large measuring cup or pitcher. (You can refrigerate the custard at this point to bake later.)

4   Pour the custard into eight ramekins or custard cups. Put the unbaked custards in a deep ovenproof pan. Fill the pan with warm water until it reaches halfway up the sides of the custard cups. Cover the pan tightly with aluminum foil and bake 45 to 50 minutes, or until the custards are just barely set. The custard will still be soft and slightly jiggly, but only in the center.

5   Remove the cooked custards from the water bath and set them on a wire cooling rack until they reach room temperature.

6   To caramelize the custards, first see the caramelization guidelines on page 200. Caramelize the ¾ cup granulated sugar in a pan on the stove using the dry method (page 202). When it has reached a dark amber color, pour some of the melted sugar directly over each of the cooled custards. Lift each custard cup while the caramel is still warm and liquid and carefully swirl it to distribute the caramel evenly over the surface. Allow a few minutes for it to harden before serving. Alternatively, caramelize the custards with a propane blowtorch, if you have one: Sprinkle each custard with 1 tablespoon white sugar. Set the torch flame at medium, and wave the tip of the flame over the sugar at close range, until the sugar begins to melt. Rotate the ramekin with your other hand for even caramelization. Continue to melt the sugar with the blowtorch until the sugar has darkened and caramelized.

COFFEE CARAMEL CUSTARD

6 SERVINGS

At Chez Panisse, we served
these custards with a dollop
of whipped cream and some
shaved chocolate, or a
sprinkle of espresso powder.
I prefer shaved chocolate
alone, although our customers
always liked the extra
whipped cream.

1¼ cups sugar
⅓ cup water
A few drops lemon juice
2½ cups cream
½ vanilla bean, split

7 egg yolks
¼ cup espresso (see Note)
Pinch of salt
½ teaspoon vanilla extract

1   Preheat the oven to 350 degrees.

2   See the caramelization guidelines on page 200. Put the sugar, water, and lemon juice in a large saucepan and place over medium heat. Use at least an 8-quart heavy saucepan to caramelize the sugar, because when you add the cream to stop the caramelization, the mixture will bubble up quite a bit before it subsides.

3   Cook the sugar until it dissolves and begins to darken. Do not stir, but it may be necessary to tilt the pan gently as the sugar caramelizes if the sugar is coloring unevenly. Continue caramelizing the sugar until it turns a dark amber color and begins to smoke. When the caramel turns a slightly deeper color, but is not burnt, remove it from the heat and *immediately* add the cream. The mixture will steam violently and bubble up, but don't be alarmed—unless you didn't take my previous advice and used a small saucepan.

4   Add the vanilla bean. Protecting your stirring hand with an oven mitt, stir the mixture with a wooden spoon, over low heat, if necessary, until the caramel is completely dissolved, and the mixture has stopped bubbling.

5   Briefly whisk the egg yolks in a separate bowl, then add some of the warm caramel cream to them, whisking constantly to prevent the yolks from cooking. Whisk in the remaining caramel cream, the espresso, salt, and vanilla. (You can refrigerate the custard at this point to bake later.)

6   Pour the custard into a large measuring cup or pitcher, and then pour into six ramekins or custard cups.

7   Put the unbaked custards in a deep ovenproof pan. Fill the pan with warm water until it reaches halfway up the sides of the custard cups. Cover the pan tightly with aluminum foil. Bake for 35 to 45 minutes, or until the custards are just barely set. The custard will still be soft and slightly jiggly, but only in the center.

8   Remove the cooked custards from the water bath and set them on a wire cooling rack for 30 minutes. Refrigerate until ready to serve.

Note: If you can't obtain freshly made espresso, substitute 1 tablespoon instant espresso powder dissolved in ¼ cup water.

NOCINO CUSTARD

8 SERVINGS

Nocino custard is the ideal way to introduce your guests to the unique flavor of nocino. The seductive green walnut essence suffuses and enhances the smooth rich custard.

2 cups heavy cream
1 cup half-and-half
½ cup plus 1 tablespoon sugar
6 egg yolks

⅛ teaspoon vanilla extract
6 to 8 tablespoons nocino
(page 173, see Note)

1   Position the oven rack in the center of the oven. Preheat the oven to 350 degrees.

2   In a saucepan, warm the cream, half-and-half, and sugar.

3   Whisk together the egg yolks in a bowl. Gradually add about one third of the warm cream mixture, whisking constantly.

4   Pour the egg mixture back into the cream in the saucepan, and stir in the vanilla and the nocino, to taste. (You can strain the mixture and refrigerate it at this point to bake later.)

5   Strain the mixture into a large measuring cup or pitcher and pour the custard into eight ramekins or custard cups.

6   Put the unbaked custards in a deep ovenproof pan. Fill the pan with warm water until it reaches halfway up the sides of the custard cups. Cover the pan tightly with aluminum foil and bake 40 to 50 minutes, or until the custards are just barely set. The custards will still be soft and slightly jiggly, but only in the center.

7   Remove the cooked custards from the water bath and set them on a wire rack to cool. Serve either warm out of the oven, or cold.

Serving suggestion: *Warm or cold, the custards are delicious served with some softly whipped cream and with shavings of chocolate or a few chopped toasted walnuts on top.*

Note: If you don't have any homemade nocino on hand, consider substituting another good nut-flavored liqueur, such as Amaretto.

BUTTERSCOTCH FLAN

8 SERVINGS

If I remember correctly, the idea for this custard was planted by Lindsey Shere. She was always suggesting desserts for me to make that merged two of our favorite flavors, caramel and butterscotch.

Flan is different from other egg custards. Because it is less rich it sets firmer and it can be unmolded onto a plate. (You can't turn out a pot de crème or a crème brûlée.) There also can be a refreshing coolness to flan that richer custards don't have.

In fact, I think this flan is best served icy-cold. In Mérida, Mexico, I enjoyed the wares of pushcart vendors whose flans were set on huge blocks of ice to keep them thoroughly chilled, a necessity in the intense blazing heat of the Yucatán.

The caramel:

¼ cup water, plus ¼ cup to stop the caramelization

¾ cup sugar

Pinch of cream of tartar or a few drops of lemon juice

The flan:

4 eggs

4 egg yolks

3 cups milk

1 cup dark brown sugar, firmly packed

1   To make the caramel: See the caramelization guidelines on page 200 before you start. Pour ¼ cup water into a heavy, medium-size skillet or saucepan, and sprinkle the sugar over it in an even layer. Cook over moderate heat, adding the cream of tartar or lemon juice when the sugar has dissolved. Do not stir at any time.

2   When the sugar begins to brown, watch it carefully. It may be necessary to tilt the pan slightly if the sugar is browning unevenly.

3   When the caramel has turned a dark reddish brown and begins to smoke, remove from the heat and quickly add the remaining ¼ cup of water.

4   The sugar will bubble up, then subside. Stir with a heatproof utensil to make sure the caramel has completely dissolved.

5   Pour the hot caramel into eight individual 4-ounce ramekins or ovenproof custard cups. Each dish should have about 1 table-spoon of caramel. Allow the caramel to harden before filling the ramekins or custard cups.

6   To make the flan: Briefly whisk together the eggs and the egg yolks in a mixing bowl. Heat the milk in a saucepan over medium heat.

7   When the milk is warm, pour it into the eggs and yolks, whisking constantly to prevent the eggs from cooking.

8   Add the brown sugar and whisk until completely dissolved. Strain the custard into a large measuring cup or pitcher. (You can refrigerate the custard at this point to bake later.)

9   Position the oven rack in the center of the oven and preheat the oven to 350 degrees. Pour the custard into the caramelized ramekins or custard cups. Put the unbaked custards in a deep ovenproof pan. Fill the pan with warm water until it reaches halfway up the sides of the custard cups. Cover tightly with aluminum foil and bake for about 35 to 45 minutes, until the custards are just barely set: still jiggly in the center, but firm around the edges. Remove the baked custards from the water bath and set them on a wire rack to cool. Refrigerate until ready to serve.

10   To unmold, run a sharp knife around the outside of the chilled custard to release it from the ramekin. Invert a serving plate over the custard, and flip over both the ramekin and the plate simultaneously. Shake a few times to release the custard and lift off the ramekin. If it is stubborn, poke the upside-down flan with your finger to release the air lock and it will slide out easily. Pour any remaining caramel from the ramekin over the flan.

Serving suggestion: *I like these served unadorned, with some nutty or spicy cookies. A heaping plate of Mexican wedding cookies (page 154) is a perfect accompaniment.*

8   Pour the hot caramel into eight individual 4-ounce ramekins or ovenproof custard cups. Each dish should have about 1 tablespoon of caramel. Allow the caramel to cool before filling the ramekins or custard cups.

9   To finish the custard: Whisk together the eggs and egg yolks in a bowl. Rewarm the milk mixture and add a small amount to the eggs, stirring constantly. Pour the warmed eggs into the flavored milk, stirring thoroughly, and strain into a pitcher or a large measuring cup. (You can refrigerate the custard at this point to bake later.)

10   Position the oven rack in the center of the oven and preheat the oven to 350 degrees. Pour the custard into the caramelized ramekins or custard cups. Put the unbaked custards in a deep ovenproof pan. Fill the pan with warm water until it reaches halfway up the sides of the custard cups. Cover the pan with aluminum foil and bake for 35 to 45 minutes, until the custards are just barely set. The custard will still be soft and slightly jiggly, but only in the center. Remove the baked custards from the water bath and set them on a wire rack to cool. Refrigerate until ready to serve.

11   To unmold, run a sharp knife around the outside of the chilled custard to release it from the ramekin. Invert a serving plate or bowl over the custard, and flip over both the ramekin and the plate simultaneously. Shake a few times to release the custard and lift off the ramekin. If it is stubborn, poke the upside-down flan with your finger to release the air lock and it will slide out easily. Pour any remaining caramel from the ramekin over the flan.

6   Remove from the oven and serve immediately, with a small pitcher of warm chocolate sauce spiked with rum to drizzle over them, or with a fruit sauce, such as raspberry.

Variations: *Try incorporating a handful of toasted and chopped pecans into the soufflé base or flavoring the base with a spicy dusting of freshly grated nutmeg. You can also make this soufflé without pastry cream for a lower-fat version or for someone with an allergy to flour. Just sweeten the mashed banana with 4 teaspoons of sugar, fold in the egg whites, and proceed as above.*

Note: Good ripe yellow bananas are a perfectly reasonable substitute if you can't find red ones.

ORANGE ALMOND BREAD PUDDING

8 TO 10 SERVINGS

When I first showed Alice Waters a list of the recipes I wanted to put in my book, she looked it over approvingly, but the first thing she said was "Where's that orange bread pudding recipe?"—so I swiftly added it to the table of contents. To my taste, this version, with its orange and almond flavors, makes a much more refined and luxurious dessert than the usual frugal bread pudding.

Variation: *A very good, extravagant variation is to make a creamy layer of chocolate at the bottom of the pudding: Just put 8 to 12 ounces coarsely broken up bittersweet chocolate in the dish before layering the bread.*

The orange custard:

2 cups milk

2 cups heavy cream

Zest of 4 oranges, peeled or grated

½ cup sugar, plus more for sprinkling on top

6 egg yolks

½ teaspoon vanilla extract

¼ teaspoon almond extract

1 tablespoon orange liqueur

½ teaspoon ground cinnamon

The almond bread pudding:

1 egg white, at room temperature

7 ounces almond paste

1 loaf of firm white bread weighing about 1 pound, sliced, crusts removed

1   To make the orange custard: Warm together the milk, cream, orange zest, and sugar. Remove from the heat, cover, and let steep until the liquid has a good orange flavor, at least 1 hour.

2   Gently beat the egg yolks, and whisk a small amount of the warm milk mixture into them. Whisk in the remaining milk mixture, vanilla and almond extracts, orange liqueur, and cinnamon. Strain the custard into a pitcher or bowl and discard the orange zest. Refrigerate the custard until you assemble the pudding.

3   To assemble the almond bread pudding: Butter a 2-quart baking dish or soufflé mold.

4   Beat together the egg white and the almond paste until smooth. Spread a spoonful of almond paste over one side of each bread slice.

5   Layer the bread slices in the baking dish, almond paste side down. If you are using a round dish, first cut the slices of bread in half diagonally, into triangles, so you can make layers of triangles arranged in a pinwheel pattern. Pour the custard over the bread and press the bread down gently, so the top layer will absorb the custard. For the bread to become completely saturated, cover and refrigerate it for an hour or as long as overnight, pressing down the bread from time to time.

6   To bake, preheat the oven to 350 degrees. Sprinkle the top of the pudding very liberally with sugar, and bake in a water bath, until the bread pudding is puffed in the center and the top has a rich golden color, about 1 hour. Serve warm.

COCONUT TAPIOCA PUDDING

8 SERVINGS

I have vivid memories of my mother's tapioca pudding cooling in a red Pyrex bowl, memories that resurfaced when I decided to devise a tapioca pudding for Monsoon restaurant. After a lot of experimentation, I came up with this recipe, which is rather like Thai sticky rice— except with tapioca.

I use the small pearl tapioca that is readily available in Asian markets. The large pearls tend to have that science-project fish-eye look that gives some people an aversion to tapioca.

3½ cups Thai coconut milk (two 13½-ounce cans)
1¾ cups milk
1 cup sugar
1 cup small pearl tapioca

Pinch of salt
1 vanilla bean, split in half lengthwise
3 eggs, separated
Vanilla extract, if necessary

1   In a medium-size heavy-bottomed saucepan (preferably non-stick), stir together the coconut milk, milk, sugar, tapioca, and salt.

2   Scrape the seeds from the split vanilla bean and add both seeds and pod to the coconut milk mixture.

3   Cook over low heat for 15 to 20 minutes, stirring constantly with a heatproof flat-edged utensil to prevent the pudding from scorching on the bottom as it thickens, until the pearls are completely cooked through and translucent. Remove from the heat.

4   Briefly stir together the egg yolks, then vigorously whisk them into the pudding, incorporating them quickly. Cool for about 10 minutes. Remove the vanilla bean.

5   Whip the egg whites until they form soft peaks and fold them into the warm pudding. Taste, and add some vanilla extract, if desired. Transfer the pudding into a bowl and refrigerate until ready to serve. Tapioca pudding will keep for 3 days in the refrigerator.

Serving suggestion: *Heap the pudding in a shallow bowl or on a platter and garnish with fresh ripe tropical fruit (mangoes, papayas, bananas, pineapples—singly or in any combination). The fruit can be served fresh or sautéed briefly with brown sugar and rum. Top with freshly grated and toasted coconut.*

Each season is a learning experience for me, since every year the fruits are different. One year the pears are sweeter and there's more of them, so you have to figure out more pear desserts. Another year the rains ruin all but a few of the cherries. It's always something different. You're forever tasting and adjusting things to suit the character of the fruit that's available.

FRUIT
DESSERTS

Fruit desserts seem to require the most flexibility of all the dishes in the dessert repertoire because you can't plan ahead. You can never be a hundred percent sure that you will be able to make a cherry tart next weekend.

One of the most challenging things at Chez Panisse was that we would always buy fruit if it was beautiful and plentiful, and our dessert menu planning would take off from there. For example, we would be confronted with cases of new citrus fruit hybrids such as Oro Blancos or Lavender Gems, and we would have to figure out what to do with them. I remember when I had just started working in the pastry department; we had a glut of red currants, and I came up with a dessert in which the currants were cooked very briefly and served over a lemon filling in a tart. I thought, Wow, this is wonderful—this is how things get invented.

Becoming familiar with fruit requires you to smell and taste constantly. I've been fortunate to live in Northern California, where we have an insatiable appetite for wonderful fruits. At Chez Panisse, people would show up at the kitchen door with foraged wild blackberries and huckleberries, with baskets of Meyer lemons from a backyard tree, with rare golden raspberries and fraises des bois, with French butter pears from a single heirloom tree—fruit so beautiful, we couldn't pass it up. No matter how busy we were, we all had to stop whatever we were doing to come and see, and we would buy, not always even bothering to ask the price. In fact, I think we became a bit of a target for a few eccentric gardeners and foragers. I suspected one gardening neighbor of deliberately waiting to deliver until just after six in the evening, when the dinner service was beginning and we were too busy to verify quantities or bargain over the price for her irresistible blackberries.

VERY SPICY CARAMEL PEARS

4 SERVINGS

Use a baking dish that will hold all of the pears in a single layer. That way they will all get thoroughly infused with the spice flavors. Adjust the spices to suit your taste— there's nothing wrong with adding a few slices of ginger, but just don't go too heavy on the star anise, which quickly becomes overwhelming. I bring the baking dish right to the table, to fill the dining room with the pears' spicy aroma. The baked pears are also good served right out of the baking dish without ever receiving the heavy cream and caramelization treatment. I often omit straining out the crushed spices since I like the way they look.

15 whole cloves
2 star anise
2 cinnamon sticks
½ teaspoon black peppercorns
4 pears, Bosc, Comice, or Butter
4 tablespoons butter (½ stick)

½ cup light or dark brown sugar, firmly packed
¼ cup Cognac, brandy, or rum
¼ cup heavy cream
Vanilla ice cream (page 121)

1   Preheat the oven to 400 degrees.

2   Coarsely crush the spices with a mortar and pestle or break them up in a plastic bag by smashing them with a rolling pin or hammer.

3   Peel and quarter the pears, and core them, slicing away the fibrous parts in the center. Cut the butter into small pieces and put them in a baking dish with the brown sugar. Put the baking dish in the oven for a few minutes to melt the butter. Arrange the pears in the baking dish, add the spices and liquor, and toss everything together so that the pears are evenly coated.

4   Cover the baking dish with foil and bake 30 to 45 minutes, until the pears are baked through. (The baking time will vary depending on the pears you use. Firm Bosc pears will take 45 minutes, but softer Comice and Butter pears will take about 30 minutes.) Remove the dish from the oven two or three times during baking, and stir the pears so they will be flavored on all sides.

5   The pears are ready when they can be easily pierced with the tip of a paring knife. Remove them from the oven and lift them out of the baking dish with a slotted spoon. Scrape the juices and spices from the baking dish into a heavy sauté pan.

6   Add the heavy cream to the pear juices and spices on the stove and cook over medium heat until the mixture turns a deep color, thickens, and caramelizes. Strain the finished caramel over the pears and serve with scoops of vanilla ice cream.

Variation: *The pears can be replaced with good, firm baking apples— peeled, cored, cut into eighths, and baked for 25 minutes.*

APPLE AND RED WINE TART

ONE 10-INCH TART; 8 SERVINGS

Soaking and cooking the apples in red wine gives them a color so brilliant that you'll gasp when you unmold this tart—my variation on the classic tart Tatin—and see the glistening red apple slices piled high. You may think 8 apples is too many, especially when you try to fit them all in the pan, but they will cook down a lot.

8 firm apples, such as Sierra Beauty, Granny Smith, or Golden Delicious

¾ cup sugar

1 bottle (750 ml) fruity red wine, preferably Zinfandel or Merlot

About 9 ounces galette dough (page 186)

Crème fraîche (page 8) or vanilla ice cream (page 121)

1   Peel and core the apples. Cut them into ¾-inch-thick slices, put them in a bowl, and toss with the sugar. Pour the red wine over them, cover, and refrigerate 24 to 48 hours. Mix them several times so that all the apples get saturated with red wine.

2   To bake the tart, position the oven rack in the center of the oven and preheat the oven to 375 degrees.

3   Drain off the red wine from the apples into a 10-inch oven-proof skillet or sauté pan. Reduce the liquid over medium-high heat until thickened and only about ⅓ cup remains. Remove from the heat and reserve a few tablespoons of the liquid to use later for glazing the finished tart. Add the apples to the pan.

4   Roll the dough on a lightly floured surface into a 14-inch circle. Drape the dough over the apples in the pan, and tuck the edges down between the skillet and the apples.

5   Bake the tart for 1 hour, or until the dough has browned and the apples are tender when poked with a paring knife. Remove from the oven and cool at least 10 minutes. Tilt the pan into the reserved syrup to drain excess liquid. Reduce to a syrupy consistency in a separate sauté pan.

6   Invert a serving dish over the tart in the pan. Wearing oven mitts, hold the skillet and the serving dish together, and simultaneously flip over the pan and the dish. As you do this, tilt the pan and dish away from you to avoid getting splashed with any hot liquid that might come out. (I do this over the sink.)

7   Lift off the sauté pan and allow the tart to cool briefly before serving. Brush with the reserved red wine syrup and serve with crème fraîche or vanilla ice cream.

PEAR, RUM, AND PECAN TART

ONE 9-INCH TART; 8 TO 10 SERVINGS

This is my favorite variation on a basic pear tart—chunky toasted pecans and sliced pears embedded in an aromatic brown butter and rum custard.

The brown butter and rum custard:

3 eggs

¼ cup flour

¾ cup granulated sugar

½ teaspoon vanilla extract

3 tablespoons dark rum

½ cup pecans, toasted

10 tablespoons (1 stick plus 2 tablespoons) butter

The pears:

2 medium pears (Bartlett, Comice, Butter, or Bosc)

2 tablespoons light or dark brown sugar, firmly packed

1 tablespoon dark rum

1 prebaked 9-inch tart shell (page 182)

Whipped cream (page192), flavored with pear eau-de-vie or dark rum

Optional: Chocolate sauce (page 196)

1   To make the brown butter and rum custard: Whisk together the eggs, flour, sugar, vanilla, and 3 tablespoons of dark rum.

2   Coarsely chop the pecans.

3   Cut the butter into large chunks. Melt it slowly over low heat in a large sauté pan or saucepan. It will bubble for a while, then settle down and stop sizzling. To protect yourself from splatters, invert a strainer over the butter while it's cooking.

4   When the butter has darkened to the color of maple syrup and smells toasty, but not burnt, remove it from the heat. Quickly pour it into the egg mixture, whisking constantly to keep it from cooking the eggs. Any sediment should remain behind in the pan, since it tastes bitter. Stir in the pecans.

5   Refrigerate the brown butter custard until chilled and thickened, about 1 hour.

6   Prepare the pears: Peel the pears, slice them in quarters, and remove the cores and the fibers that run down the center. Cut each quarter lengthwise into ¼-inch-thick slices. Put them in a mixing bowl with the brown sugar and 1 tablespoon dark rum.

Macerate for at least 15 minutes, tossing frequently to coat the slices.

7   To bake the tart, position the oven rack in the center of the oven and preheat the oven to 375 degrees.

8   Arrange the pear slices concentrically in the prebaked tart shell. Pour the brown butter custard over the pears. Fill the tart to the rim, but do not overfill it. Depending on the size of the pears, you may have some brown butter custard left over.

9   Set the unbaked tart on a baking sheet, and bake for 30 minutes, until browned. Cool completely before serving.

Serving suggestion: *Serve with whipped cream flavored with pear eau-de-vie or dark rum and perhaps with a little chocolate sauce dribbled around.*

Note: The flavors of this tart continue to improve for several hours after the tart has cooled.

5   When the surface of the crêpe is covered with small bubble holes, lift the edge of the crêpe with the butter knife. With your fingers (or a spatula), lift up the crêpe and flip it over. Cook the other side for 30 seconds or so, until it has browned.

6   Turn the finished crêpe out onto a dinner plate and immediately add another 2 tablespoons of batter to start the next crêpe. Stir the batter between crêpes to keep it homogenous: Otherwise, since flour tends to sink, the batter at the bottom of the bowl will be too thick. Keep frying until all the crêpes have been cooked, then wrap them in plastic wrap and refrigerate them until ready to use. They can also be frozen at this point.

7   To make the Calvados butter: Beat together the butter, powdered sugar, Calvados, and vanilla.

8   To assemble and finish the crêpes: Spread about 2 teaspoons of the Calvados butter over one quarter of one side of each crêpe. Fold the crêpe over, making a half circle, then fold over again so you have a quarter circle.

9   Slice the apples in ½-inch-thick slices. Melt 1 tablespoon butter in a large sauté pan over medium heat (I use a 14-inch nonstick sauté pan), add the apple slices, and cook until they begin to soften, stirring occasionally. Add 1½ tablespoons sugar and continue cooking, stirring less frequently, until the apples begin to caramelize and are mostly cooked through.

10   Transfer the apples to a bowl and add the apple cider to the pan. Add the remaining 2 tablespoons sugar, increase the heat, and reduce the cider by half.

11   Reduce the heat and arrange the butter-filled crêpes in the pan with the cider. Return the cooked apples to the pan. Reduce the heat, add the Calvados and vanilla, and simmer for about a minute to heat the crêpes and apples, until the sauce has thickened slightly. Serve immediately.

Note: Apple brandy, applejack, and Cognac make good substitutes if Calvados is not available.

APPLE AND FRANGIPANE GALETTE

6 TO 8 SERVINGS

This is a seasonal favorite at Chez Panisse, since most people find a warm apple tart irresistible in autumn. This galette is very rustic, although the frangipane makes it a bit more refined.

Use full-flavored apples that will hold up in the tart. Varieties I've used successfully for baking include Sierra Beauty, Granny Smith, Cortland, Pippin, and Golden Delicious, but you may have another favorite that will work just fine. Pink Pearl is an especially gorgeous apple for this galette if you're lucky enough to live near a grower who specializes in unusual apple varieties.

6 apples (about 2 pounds)
About 9 ounces galette dough (page 186)
1 cup frangipane (page 189)
2 tablespoons butter, melted

3 tablespoons sugar
Optional: Calvados, Cognac, or honey
Crème fraîche (page 8) or vanilla ice cream (page 121)

1   Peel, core, and slice the apples into ½-inch-thick slices.

2   Position the oven rack in the center of the oven and preheat the oven to 375 degrees.

3   On a lightly floured surface, roll the dough into a circle approximately 14 inches in diameter. Transfer it onto a baking sheet that has been lined with parchment paper.

4   Smear the frangipane over the dough, leaving a 2-inch border. Arrange the apple slices concentrically over the frangipane or scatter them in an even layer. Fold the border of the crust back over the apples and brush the crust with the melted butter. Sprinkle 2 tablespoons of the sugar over the crust, and the remaining tablespoon of sugar over the apples.

5   Bake the tart for 1 hour, until the apples are cooked and the crust is browned. Slide the tart off the sheet pan, remove the parchment paper, and cool briefly on a wire rack. Serve, perhaps drizzled with Calvados, Cognac, or honey, and with a spoonful of crème fraîche or vanilla ice cream.

POACHED FRUIT COMPOTE

Poaching fruit is a way of enhancing the flavors of both fresh and dried fruits. Especially in the fall and winter months, when the selection of fresh fruit is more restricted, poaching dried fruits lends a welcome variety to your dessert choices. Poaching fresh fruit can add flavor to fruit that may be underripe or too imperfect to serve raw. Poaching fruit can also preserve fresh fruit for a short period of time if you are deluged with a lot of ripe fruit all at once.

My poached fruit compotes are all the same—and never the same twice. I make a syrup of one part sugar to four parts liquid (either all water or a mixture of red or white wine and water). I may flavor it with any number of things: a few sprigs of thyme or rosemary; whole spices such as allspice berries, cinnamon sticks, star anise, cloves, or peppercorns; slices of fresh ginger; crushed bitter almonds; a split vanilla bean; tea leaves (wrapped in cheesecloth or in a tea ball); and lemon or orange zest.

I tend to poach fruits that are not highly flavorful, such as Bosc pears or apples, in something rather bold, such as a red or white wine syrup flavored with fresh ginger and a cinnamon stick. Dried fruits such as apricots, prunes, raisins, and sour cherries may want no more than a few strips of lemon zest added to their poaching syrup. Poaching tends to concentrate flavors, so be judicious in your use of flavorings. Star anise and fresh ginger, for example, can be overwhelming if more than a few pieces are added.

Always begin by bringing your poaching syrup to a boil with the spices or flavorings. Then add your fruit and cook over very low heat so the fruit doesn't cook too quickly on the outside, or overcook and fall apart. Make enough syrup to cover the fruit by at least an inch. Cover the poaching fruit with a round of parchment paper and press down on it from time to time to ensure that the fruit cooks evenly.

Cook only until the fruit is done, which will vary considerably, depending on ripeness and firmness. Pears, for example, will turn translucent, and can cook in as little as 15 minutes, especially if they are sliced first. Quince slices turn a lovely, brilliant shade of pink, and usually take at least an hour to cook. Dried fruits, such as prunes and apricots, soften and lose their chewiness. You should always poach fruits separately, unless they are of similar texture. For example, poached apples will cook far more quickly than dried apricots, while dried apricots and dried prunes can be poached together.

mixture into the egg yolks and then scrape the warmed egg yolk mixture into the saucepan.

6   Keep cooking and stirring the custard until it comes to a boil again. It will become quite thick and mound up like mayonnaise. Remove it from the heat and strain it into the butterscotch. Add the rum and vanilla and whisk until the butterscotch has dissolved into the custard.

7   Slice the bananas into ½-inch-thick slices and scatter them over the bottom of the baked cookie crust. Pour the custard over, cover with plastic wrap, and refrigerate until chilled.

8   Make the whipped cream topping: When it's time to serve the pie, whip the cream until it just begins to mound up softly, add the sugar, rum, and vanilla extract, and keep whisking until the cream holds soft peaks. Spread or pipe the topping over the pie. Decorate the pie with chocolate shavings.

Note: To make chocolate shavings, use a vegetable peeler to shave curls of chocolate in long strokes from a block of milk or bittersweet chocolate.

PINEAPPLE, RHUBARB, AND RASPBERRY COBBLER

8 SERVINGS

Why this unusual combination of pineapple, rhubarb, and raspberries? Well, it was early in the springtime, and there wasn't much at the market except for rhubarb and some delicious fresh pineapples from Maui—and there were some of last summer's raspberries in the freezer. It turned out to be so delicious that even rhubarb haters liked it. I would definitely make it for company the next time the ingredients converge in my kitchen.

Despite the evidence of the accompanying picture, this recipe makes 8 biscuits. They're so good that someone couldn't resist sneaking one for breakfast before the cobbler photo was taken!

The filling:
2 pounds rhubarb (7 cups, sliced)

½ pineapple, peeled, cored, and eyes removed (2 cups, cubed)

One 1-pint basket raspberries (2 cups)

2 tablespoons flour

¾ cup sugar

1 teaspoon vanilla extract

1 tablespoon kirsch

The biscuits:
3 cups flour

1½ teaspoons salt

2 tablespoons sugar

1 tablespoon baking powder

10 tablespoons (1 stick plus 2 tablespoons) butter, chilled

¾ cup to 1 cup heavy cream or buttermilk

1 egg yolk

1 teaspoon milk

Vanilla ice cream (page 121)

1   Position the oven rack in the center of the oven and preheat the oven to 400 degrees.

2   To make the filling: Wash the rhubarb and trim off both ends of the stalks. Cut into ½-inch slices. Cut the pineapple into ½-inch cubes.

3   Mix together the rhubarb, pineapple, and raspberries with the flour, sugar, vanilla, and kirsch.

4   Transfer the fruit to a shallow 2-quart baking dish, and bake for 40 minutes, stirring the fruit several times during baking.

5   While the fruit bakes, make the biscuits: Sift together the flour, salt, sugar, and baking powder.

6   Cut the butter into ½-inch cubes and add to the dry ingredients. Mix briefly until the butter is mostly incorporated but small chunks are still visible. Mix in ¾ cup heavy cream or buttermilk, then gather the dough into a ball with your hands. If the dough is too dry, add more liquid until you can gather it together.

7   Roll out the dough on a lightly floured surface until it is ¾ inch thick. With a biscuit cutter (either a 3-inch round or any appropriate shape) dipped in flour, cut out 8 biscuits. You may

need to gather the dough scraps and roll them out again in order to make all 8 biscuits.

8   Remove the fruit from the oven and place the biscuits on top. Mix together the egg yolk and milk and brush the tops of the biscuits with the egg wash.

9   Return the cobbler to the oven and continue baking for 15 to 20 minutes, until the biscuits have browned. This cobbler must be served with vanilla ice cream!

BUTTERNUT SQUASH PIE

ONE 10-INCH PIE

After years of making both pumpkin and butternut squash pies, I've decided that butternut squash makes the better pie. I like the sweet, intense orange pulp of butternut squash, and to me it has a superior flavor.

Note that the filling is added still warm to the prebaked pie shell. This reduces the baking time for the pie and eliminates the cumbersome necessity of using strips of aluminum foil to keep the rim of the crust from burning while the custard inside finishes baking. I first tried this technique when I was faced with an onslaught of pie orders one especially busy Halloween at Chez Panisse.

2 pounds butternut squash (to make about 2 cups pulp)

1 cup heavy cream

½ cup milk

4 eggs

¾ cup light brown sugar, firmly packed

1 teaspoon ground ginger

1 teaspoon ground cinnamon

¼ teaspoon ground cloves

¼ teaspoon ground black pepper

¼ teaspoon grated nutmeg

Pinch of salt

½ teaspoon vanilla extract

1 tablespoon Cognac or brandy

One 10-inch prebaked pie shell (page 184)

Whipped cream (page 192) flavored with brandy

1   Position the oven rack in the center of the oven and preheat the oven to 400 degrees. Line a baking sheet with parchment paper and rub generously with butter.

2   Slice the butternut squash in half lengthwise. With a spoon, remove the seeds and fibers from the cavity and place the halves on the buttered baking sheet, cut side down. Bake for 45 minutes, or until the squash is tender and fully cooked.

3   While the squash is baking, mix together the cream, milk, eggs, sugar, all the spices, salt, vanilla, and Cognac or brandy.

4   When the squash is cooked, remove it from the oven and turn the oven down to 375 degrees. Scoop out the squash pulp and add to the other ingredients. Mix until smooth in a blender or food processor.

5   Pour the warm filling into the prebaked pie shell and bake for 30 to 35 minutes. The pie should be slightly jiggly, and just barely set in the center. (An overcooked pie will crack when cooling.) Some people like this pie warm, but I prefer it cold served with brandy-flavored whipped cream.

Note: You can make the filling up to 2 days in advance and keep it in the refrigerator. Warm it slowly on the stove top, stirring constantly, before filling the pie shell.

BLUEBERRY COMPOTE

4 SERVINGS

Eating blueberries is one of summer's fleeting pleasures. If you are lucky enough to live where there are wild blueberries or huckleberries, use them instead. The rest of us will have to be content with cultivated blueberries. My earliest lesson in disappointment began when my dad planted some blueberry shrubs next to our house in New England. Every single year after that, just as the greenish berries started to ripen, the birds would come and eat them all. Year after year we watched those bushes and not once were we able to gather any of the berries for ourselves.

One 1-pint basket blueberries (2 cups)

⅓ cup sugar

Grated zest of 1 lemon

2 tablespoons water

1 teaspoon tapioca flour or cornstarch

2 tablespoons lemon juice, or more to taste

Optional: Meyer lemon sorbet (page 111)

1   In a nonreactive saucepan, heat the blueberries with the sugar, lemon zest, and water until the blueberries soften and release their liquid.

2   Dissolve the tapioca flour or cornstarch in the lemon juice and add to the blueberries. Cook until the berry mixture begins to boil.

3   Remove from the heat, cool slightly, and serve, preferably with Meyer lemon sorbet.

BLUEBERRY AND WHITE CHOCOLATE TART

ONE 9-INCH TART

Because I find the flavor of blueberries somewhat delicate, I enjoy them most when they are paired with a single accompanying flavor. White chocolate makes a lovely, surprisingly harmonious accompaniment to blueberries, and the custard filling helps control the chaos of tumbling blueberries when you slice into the tart.

The white chocolate custard:

1 teaspoon powdered gelatin

2 tablespoons cold water

4 ounces white chocolate

½ cup milk

¼ teaspoon vanilla extract

2 egg yolks

⅔ cup heavy cream, softly beaten

2 tablespoons kirsch

1 prebaked 9-inch tart shell (page 182), cooled to room temperature

The blueberry topping:

Two 1-pint baskets blueberries (4 cups)

2 tablespoons water

2 tablespoons sugar

Juice of ½ lemon

1   To make the white chocolate custard: In a large bowl, dissolve the gelatin by sprinkling it over the cold water. Let it stand 5 minutes.

2   Chop the white chocolate into smallish pieces and add to the bowl with the gelatin.

3   Warm the milk in a saucepan with the vanilla extract.

4   Stir together the egg yolks in a bowl and gradually whisk in a small amount of the warmed milk.

5   Transfer the warmed egg yolks into the saucepan with the rest of the milk, and cook over low heat, stirring with a heatproof spatula, until the mixture has thickened just enough to coat it (170 degrees). Immediately strain the custard through a fine sieve into the bowl containing the white chocolate and gelatin. Stir continuously until the white chocolate has completely melted and the gelatin is dissolved. Cool to room temperature. You can speed the cooling by placing the bowl in a larger bowl of ice.

6   Once the white chocolate custard has cooled, whip the cream until it just begins to form soft peaks. Add the kirsch.

7   Fold the kirsch whipped cream into the white chocolate custard, pour into the cooled, prebaked tart shell, and refrigerate to set for at least 1 hour or for as long as overnight if you wish.

8   Make the blueberry topping: Put one fourth of the blueberries (½ pint) in a saucepan with the water, sugar, and lemon juice. Mash the blueberries with a spatula and cook over low heat, stir-

ring occasionally, until the mixture has cooked down and thickened somewhat. There should be about 1/3 cup of this jam. Cool.

9   Stir the rest of the blueberries into the jam. Spoon the blueberry topping over the chilled tart. Serve immediately.

PAVLOVA

I wish I could say I never saw this, but my friend Joanne Weir, who teaches cooking in Australia, once brought me back a plastic egg that looked like it housed a pair of supermarket pantyhose. Instead, the egg encapsulated a mix for Pavlova, a dessert much loved by Australians.

Traditionally, Pavlova is no more than a meringue topped with whipped cream and tropical fruit. Because of its base of easily broken meringue, and the cream and fruit on top, a big Pavlova is almost impossible to slice and serve. I prefer serving individual ones, which are neater and more fun: Each guest gets an individual creation.

The meringues (4 to serve, plus 1 tester meringue):

3 egg whites, at room temperature

Pinch of cream of tartar

2/3 cup sugar

1/2 teaspoon vanilla extract

The assembly:

1 pint strawberry mango sorbet (page 109)

1/2 cup heavy cream, softly whipped, unsweetened, with a few drops vanilla extract

About 2 cups tropical fruits: any combination of peeled and sliced pineapple, mango, papaya, kiwi, and bananas; halved litchis; sliced kumquats and strawberries; passion fruit pulp; and orange segments

Blackberry sauce (page 198) or raspberry sauce (page 198), or both

1   To make the meringues: Position the oven rack in the center of the oven and preheat the oven to 200 degrees.

2   With an electric mixer, whip the egg whites until they become frothy. Add the cream of tartar and continue whipping until the whites begin to hold their shape and form soft, drooping peaks when you lift the whip. Keep beating the egg whites, gradually whisking in the sugar. Add the vanilla. Whip the meringue at high speed until it is shiny and forms stiff peaks.

3   Drop the meringue in five equal mounds, spaced evenly, on a parchment-lined baking sheet. With the spatula or the back of a soup spoon, roughly flatten the meringue to a diameter of 4 to 5 inches, and about 1/2 inch high. Then make a depression in the center of the meringue, like the gravy well in mashed potatoes, which will eventually hold the cream and fruits.

4   Dry the meringues in the oven for about 1 1/2 hours. Turn off the heat and leave the meringues in the oven to dry for at least 1 more hour. They may take longer, depending on your oven. Test a meringue by taking one out of the oven, letting it cool, and breaking it. It should break crisply all the way through, with no softness or resistance.

5   Cool the meringues completely at room temperature and store in an airtight container until ready to serve.

6   To assemble the Pavlovas: Place each meringue on a plate.
Scoop some sorbet into the center of the meringue. Plop a heaping spoonful of the whipped cream next to the sorbet and scatter
the fruit over and around the sides of the meringue. Spoon fruit
sauce over and around the fruits.

TROPICAL FRUIT SOUP

4 SERVINGS

I often made this dessert when I was the pastry chef of Monsoon, the pan-Asian San Francisco restaurant where I was charged with inventing desserts that used the flavors of Asian cuisines. I would surround myself with bowls of tropical fruits, expertly sliced just before the first diners arrived. When someone ordered tropical fruit soup, I carefully arranged the fruit in a bowl, ladling over some of the cold soup base that I kept on ice nearby. To finish the presentation, I would add a big, perfect scoop of coconut sherbet, a scattering of freshly torn mint leaves, and a shard of coconut meringue or, sometimes, a large crispy cookie. Then it was off to the dining room.

Use whatever combination of fruits you like. Visit your nearest ethnic market and experiment with any unusual

The soup base:

2 cups water

2/3 cup sugar

1/2 cinnamon stick

1/2 star anise

8 whole cloves

8 black peppercorns

1/4 vanilla bean

Zest of 2 oranges, peeled or grated

2 pieces lemongrass, 2 inches long, sliced (use the white part from the root end)

4 thin slices fresh ginger

1 tablespoon dark rum

The coconut meringue:

1 egg white, at room temperature

Pinch of salt

1/4 cup sugar

1/2 cup unsweetened dried coconut

The assembly:

About 2 cups tropical fruits: any combination of peeled and sliced pineapple, mango, papaya, kiwi, and bananas; halved litchis; sliced kumquats and strawberries; passion fruit pulp; and orange segments

Sugar, as necessary

Fresh mint to garnish the soup

1 pint coconut sherbet (page 118)

1   To make the fruit soup base: Bring the water and sugar to a boil. Meanwhile, coarsely crush the cinnamon, star anise, cloves, and black peppercorns in a mortar, or put them in a plastic bag and crush them with a rolling pin or a hammer. Add the spices to the boiling syrup, turn off the heat, and add the vanilla bean, orange zest, lemongrass, and ginger. Cover the pan, and steep for 1 hour or more.

2   Strain the soup base and discard the flavorings. Add the rum and chill thoroughly.

3   Position the oven rack in the center of the oven and preheat the oven to 350 degrees.

4   To make the meringue: Whip the egg white with the salt slowly until it is frothy, then increase your speed, whisking until the white stands in firm but drooping peaks.

tropical fruit you might find there. Don't be put off if the soup base tastes strangely spicy. Combined with the tropical fruits and the coconut sherbet, the flavors work. I have also served this with other fruit sorbets with great success. Chill the serving bowls so everything stays refreshingly icy cold.

5   Continue to whip the whites as you sprinkle the sugar over them. Keep whipping until all the sugar has been added and the meringue is stiff and shiny. Fold in the coconut.

6   Spread the coconut meringue into a very thin layer on a parchment-lined baking sheet, ideally with an offset metal spatula. The meringue should measure about 10 by 13 inches, spread quite thinly.

7   Bake for 10 minutes, until deep golden brown.

8   After the meringue has cooled completely, lift it off the baking sheet, still attached to the paper, and carefully turn it over. Hold the sheet of meringue in place as you gently peel the parchment from the back of the meringue. If you try to lift the meringue away from the paper, it can break into little pieces; instead, you must pull the paper away from the meringue. Break the meringue into large shards and store them in an airtight container until you assemble the dessert. (They will keep for up to a week.)

9   To assemble the fruit soup: Toss all the prepared fruits together in a bowl. Taste for sweetness, and add a sprinkling of sugar if they are too tart.

10   Divide the fruits into four wide soup bowls and ladle the chilled soup base over them.

11   Tear some mint leaves into tiny pieces and scatter them over the soup. Place a scoop of the coconut sherbet in the center and stick a shard of the coconut meringue into the top of the sherbet.

The nomenclature can be a little confusing: Ice creams and *gelati,* the Italian-style ice creams, are the richest of the frozen desserts. Sherbets, which are lighter, still may contain egg whites and milk. The sorbets (a French word) consist of fruit (juice or purée) and sugar frozen together. All of these are made in an ice cream freezer, which keeps the mixture in motion so that it freezes smoothly without ice crystallization spoiling the texture. The frozen nougat is an anomaly: a frozen confection of praline, pistachios, egg whites, and cream that you can make without an ice cream freezer.

The gelées (another French borrowing that means "things that have jelled") are something different again, all fruit- or wine-flavored gelatin desserts—not frozen, but chilled.

Frozen desserts are best served slightly softened, taken out of the freezer and allowed to approach the melting point. And remember that all it takes to make an ice cream sandwich is scoopable ice cream or sherbet and 2 excellent cookies. Try Flo's chocolate snaps (page 143) sandwiched around mint sherbet, or gingersnaps (page 144) enveloping vanilla ice cream.

TANGERINE OR PASSION FRUIT SORBET

ABOUT 1 QUART

The sweet, tangy flavor of tangerine sorbet is an excellent end to a rich dinner. For a special occasion, save the juiced and scraped-out tangerine halves or passion fruit shells, and fill them with scoops of the just-frozen sherbet, rounding and smoothing the tops to resemble the fruits themselves.

Because citrus juice contains a great deal of water, I add some liquor to the sorbet mix to keep the frozen sherbet slightly soft and easy to scoop. You can eliminate it, or increase the amount a bit to suit your taste.

4 cups tangerine or tangelo juice (about 10 tangerines), or 3 cups tangerine juice and 1 cup passion fruit pulp (about 12 passion fruits)

1 cup sugar

¼ cup Champagne, or 2 tablespoons vodka

1   Mix 1 cup of the tangerine juice with the sugar and heat in a nonreactive saucepan until the sugar has completely dissolved.

2   Add the remaining juice (or juice and passion fruit pulp) and the Champagne or vodka. Chill thoroughly, then freeze in an ice cream maker according to the manufacturer's instructions.

Note: Fresh passion fruit is sold at well-stocked supermarkets, and excellent-quality frozen passion fruit pulp can also be found. If you use fresh passion fruit, save a few of the seeds and mix them into the sherbet just after it has been frozen.

BLACKBERRY SORBET

ABOUT 1 QUART

Whenever I pick a bucket of ripe wild blackberries along the roadsides of nearby Sonoma County, I make this sorbet—so shiny and dark, it's almost inky. Blackberries that are dead ripe are fragrant and sweet, while underripe blackberries are quite tart. If you gather your own, you'll undoubtedly taste a few while you pick and figure out which are which without needing further instruction or encouragement from me.

I always like to leave a few seeds in the purée—that way people know you used real blackberries and made the sorbet yourself—and I like to serve it with scoops of vanilla ice cream (page 121), too.

Four 1-pint baskets blackberries (8 cups)
1 cup sugar

1 cup water
2 teaspoons lemon juice
2 teaspoons kirsch (or vodka)

1   Purée the blackberries in a food processor and force the purée through a sieve to remove most of the seeds. Or pass the berries through a food mill fitted with a fine disk.

2   Heat the sugar and the water until the sugar dissolves. Stir this syrup into the blackberry purée.

3   Stir in the lemon juice and kirsch. Taste and adjust the flavoring, adding more lemon juice and kirsch if desired.

4   Freeze in an ice cream maker according to the manufacturer's instructions.

BLANCO Y NEGRO

4 SERVINGS (ABOUT 1 QUART SHERBET)

Blanco y negro is a summertime pleasure, and something simple that tastes terrific. It reminds me of those chilled coffee drinks so popular at coffee bars—utterly refreshing, and especially welcome when it's really hot outside. Be ready to make more espresso; you and your guests will probably want second helpings.

The lemon-cinnamon sherbet:

4 cups milk

¾ cup sugar

Grated zest of 2 lemons

2 cinnamon sticks, coarsely crushed

The espresso and assembly:

1 to 2 teaspoons sugar

½ cup warm espresso

Optional: Chopped candied lemon peel (page 197)

1   To make the lemon-cinnamon sherbet: Warm the milk and sugar in a nonreactive saucepan.

2   Add the lemon zest and cinnamon. Remove from the heat, cover, and steep for 2 hours or until the flavor is sufficiently strong.

3   Strain the mixture and discard the zest and cinnamon. Chill the sherbet mixture thoroughly. Freeze in an ice cream maker according to the manufacturer's instructions.

4   To make the espresso and assemble: First dissolve the sugar in the warm espresso, using either 1 or 2 teaspoons, according to your preference. Scoop two or three mounds of the lemon-cinnamon sherbet into stemmed glasses or small deep bowls. Pour 2 tablespoons of the sweetened espresso over each serving of the sherbet. Although it's not necessary, a good garnish is a small amount of chopped candied lemon peel.

WHITE NECTARINE SORBET WITH BLACKBERRIES IN PLUM WINE IN A FIVE-SPICE COOKIE CUP

6 TO 8 SERVINGS (ABOUT 1 QUART SORBET)

Having worked with Bruce Cost, an Asian food scholar, chef, and purist, I've developed a distaste for much of the so-called "Pacific Rim cuisine." Too often the cross-cultural combinations are so outlandish and slapdash that the food tastes more like Pacific whim cuisine. Nevertheless, there are always exceptions, and this is one. The cookie cups with that distinctively Chinese five-spice flavor go perfectly with the sorbet, the berries, and the plum wine. The title of this dessert is fussy, the preparation is easy.

Although five-spice powder is available premixed in Asian groceries—some formulas with more than five spices!—the commercial mixtures are often stale and lack the punchy blast of flavor you get when you make your own.

The white nectarine sorbet:

9 small white nectarines (about 1½ pounds); (yellow nectarines can be substituted)

⅓ cup plus ½ cup water

¾ cup sugar

Optional: Lemon juice or kirsch, to taste

The five-spice cookie cups:

4 tablespoons (½ stick) butter, at room temperature

⅓ cup sugar

2 egg whites, at room temperature

⅓ cup flour

1 teaspoon ground cinnamon

1 teaspoon ground ginger

½ teaspoon ground cloves

⅛ teaspoon ground star anise

½ teaspoon ground Sichuan pepper

The blackberries in plum wine:

1½ cups plum wine

One 1-pint basket blackberries (2 cups)

2 tablespoons sugar

Toasted sliced almonds or sesame seeds for garnish

1 To make the white nectarine sorbet: Rinse and halve the nectarines. Remove the pits and cut the halves into ½-inch-thick slices. Crack open a few of the pits with a hammer and remove the almondlike kernels.

2 In a nonreactive saucepan, cook the nectarine slices and kernels with the ⅓ cup of water, covered, over medium heat, stirring occasionally, until the nectarines are fully cooked, about 10 to 15 minutes.

3 Purée the cooked nectarines with the sugar and the remaining ½ cup of water in either a food processor or a blender. (If using a blender, for safety, do not fill it more than half full with hot fruit.) If you wish, add lemon juice or kirsch to taste. Refrigerate the sorbet mixture completely before freezing, then freeze in an ice cream maker according to the manufacturer's instructions.

4 To make the cookie cups: Position the oven rack in the center of the oven and preheat the oven to 350 degrees.

VANILLA ICE CREAM

ABOUT 1 QUART

This is my basic vanilla ice cream recipe. Allthough here it's infused with vanilla bean, you can leave it out and flavor the custard with a few tablespoons of liquor instead—rum, Cognac, bourbon, or, a favorite of mine, Chartreuse. Try my favorite combination: the ice cream custard flavored with a couple of shots of espresso, frozen, and served with warm chocolate sauce. If you like very rich ice cream, substitute half-and-half for the milk.

1 cup milk
Pinch of salt
¾ cup sugar
1 vanilla bean

5 egg yolks
2 cups heavy cream
¼ teaspoon vanilla extract

1   Measure the milk, salt, and sugar into a saucepan. Split the vanilla bean lengthwise and scrape the seeds into the milk with the tip of a paring knife. Add the vanilla bean pod to the milk and heat the mixture until it begins to simmer.

2   Stir together the egg yolks in a bowl and gradually add some of the warmed milk, stirring constantly as you pour. Pour the warmed yolks back into the saucepan.

3   Cook over low heat, stirring constantly and scraping the bottom with a heat-resistant spatula, until the custard thickens enough to coat the spatula. Strain the custard into the heavy cream and add the vanilla extract. Put the vanilla bean back into the custard and cream to continue steeping. Chill thoroughly, then remove the vanilla bean and freeze in an ice cream maker according to the manufacturer's instructions.

WHITE CHOCOLATE–GINGER ICE CREAM WITH CHOCOLATE-COVERED PEANUTS

ABOUT 1 QUART

I served homemade ice cream cones filled with this ice cream at Cuisines of the Sun, an annual event where guest chefs show off for an audience of food lovers at a resort hotel on the big island of Hawaii. The occasion was an outdoor reception for hundreds of the well-fed (and well-heeled) attendees, dressed incongruously in loud aloha shirts and muumuus. (The crispy cones were made from the sesame orange almond tuile recipe on page 156.) No one turned down an ice cream cone. After all, what could be better after a long day spent idly lounging on the beach?

The white chocolate–ginger ice cream:

One 3-inch piece fresh ginger (about 2½ ounces)
½ cup sugar
1 cup milk
1 cup plus 1 cup heavy cream

7 ounces white chocolate
4 egg yolks

The chocolate-covered peanuts:

1 cup peanuts
5 ounces bittersweet chocolate

1   To make the white chocolate–ginger ice cream: Slice the ginger thin, cover it with water in a saucepan, bring to a boil, and cook for 2 minutes. Drain away the water, leaving the blanched ginger in the pan. Add the sugar, milk, and 1 cup of heavy cream and heat the mixture until it begins to simmer. Remove from the heat, cover, and steep for at least an hour, or until you are satisfied with the ginger flavor.

2   Chop the white chocolate and put it in a large bowl.

3   In a separate bowl, whisk together the egg yolks, then gradually add some of the ginger-infused cream mixture, whisking constantly as you pour in the warm cream. Pour the warmed egg yolks back into the saucepan.

4   Cook over low heat, stirring constantly and scraping the bottom with a heat-resistant spatula, until the custard thickens enough to coat the spatula. Strain the custard into the white chocolate, and stir until the chocolate is completely melted. Add the remaining 1 cup of heavy cream and chill thoroughly while you make the chocolate-covered peanuts.

5   To make the chocolate-covered peanuts: Preheat the oven to 350 degrees. Toast the peanuts for 10 minutes, until deep golden brown. Cool. Roughly chop the bittersweet chocolate and melt it in a clean, dry bowl set over a pan of simmering water. Cover a baking sheet with parchment paper or plastic wrap.

6   Once the chocolate has melted, add the peanuts. Stir until they are completely coated with chocolate, then spread the coated peanuts in an even layer on the baking sheet.

7   When the chocolate-covered peanuts have hardened, chop them into bite-sized pieces.

8   Freeze the chilled custard in an ice cream freezer according to the manufacturer's instructions, then fold in the chocolate-covered peanuts.

Serving suggestion: *At home, I often serve tall glasses of green tea with this ice cream.*

CARAMEL ICE CREAM

ABOUT 1 QUART

The first time I had caramel ice cream, I was at Berthillon in Paris, known far and wide for having the best ice cream anywhere. As I walked away from the counter, I took a bite. I stopped dead in my tracks and stood there on the sidewalk, speechless with awe at the incredible caramel flavor. (As those who know me can attest, I am seldom speechless.) When I got back home, I practiced making caramel ice cream until I got it to taste as good as it did in Paris.

Use your imagination with caramel ice cream. Toasted nuts, praline, leftover chocolate brownies, broken cookies, bits of chocolate—these all are worthwhile things to fold into the just-frozen custard. I have a particular fondness for a swirl of chocolate sauce (page 196) mixed into caramel ice cream. Be sure not to overmix when adding the chocolate sauce or you will muddy the swirl effect.

1½ cups sugar	1½ cups half-and-half
1 vanilla bean, split	¼ teaspoon salt
2 cups heavy cream	6 egg yolks

1   See the caramelization guidelines on page 200. Sprinkle an even layer of the sugar into a heavy medium-size saucepan (at least 2 quarts). Add the vanilla bean and heat the sugar until it begins to liquefy around the edges. As the sugar melts, occasionally give it a gentle stir with a wood or heat-resistant spatula to prevent it from burning in any one spot.

2   Once the sugar has begun to darken, it will cook very quickly. When the edges begin to bubble and the amber-colored sugar has begun to smoke, remove from the heat and quickly pour in the heavy cream, stirring to dissolve the caramel. The mixture will steam considerably when you add the cream and possibly bubble up. You may want to cover you hands with oven mitts first.

3   Whisk the half-and-half and the salt into the caramel cream. Lightly whisk together the egg yolks in a bowl and gradually add the caramel cream, whisking constantly as you pour in the hot liquid. The mixture may look slightly curdled now, but it will smooth out later.

4   Strain the caramel ice cream base into a container and chill thoroughly. Freeze in an ice cream maker according to the manufacturer's instructions.

Note: It isn't necessary to cook the custard on the stove, as it is for other ice cream recipes, because the yolks are sufficiently heated by the caramel cream poured over them.

Variation: *I often substitute crème fraîche for up to half of the cream in this recipe. If you do the same, be sure to cool and freeze the ice cream mixture within a few hours. If you leave it overnight, even when refrigerated, the crème fraîche culture's continuing activity may make the mixture too sour.*

CHOCOLATE GELATO

ABOUT 1 QUART OF GELATO

I am constantly asked about the difference between ice cream and gelato. Gelato has a richer, more concentrated flavor than regular ice cream, and generally has both less fat and less air (which is referred to as "overrun" in the business). Gelato takes a little longer to freeze and will not freeze as firm as American ice cream. It should resemble very thick pudding.

This chocolate gelato, my favorite, was inspired by a recipe of Marcella Hazan's. I always enjoy watching people as they take their first bite and seeing their shock give way to ravishment as they are seduced by the intensity of the chocolate. Serve chocolate gelato as an Italian sundae in little footed bowls, topped with spoonfuls of whipped cream, a few candied cherries (page 179) with some of their syrup, and a scattering of toasted sliced almonds.

½ cup Dutch-process cocoa
2 cups milk
5 ounces bittersweet chocolate

¾ cup sugar
4 egg yolks

1   Whisk the cocoa with 1 cup of the milk in a saucepan. Bring to a boil over moderate heat. Remove from the heat. Coarsely chop the chocolate and stir it into the cocoa mixture until it has completely melted.

2   In another saucepan, warm the remaining 1 cup of milk with the sugar.

3   Whisk together the egg yolks in a bowl and gradually pour in some of the warmed milk and sugar, whisking constantly as you pour. Pour the warmed egg mixture back into the saucepan.

4   Cook over low to moderate heat, constantly stirring and scraping the bottom, until the custard thickens enough to coat the spatula. Strain the custard into the chocolate mixture and mix well. Chill thoroughly, then freeze in an ice cream maker according to the manufacturer's instructions.

MEXICAN CHOCOLATE ICE CREAM

ABOUT 1 QUART

Every time I put this ice cream on the menu, Chez Panisse café chef Gilbert Pilgram would remind me that nothing in particular about this ice cream is authentically Mexican—unlike Gilbert himself, who grew up in Mexico City. Perhaps not, but it reminds me of the cylindrical paper-wrapped blocks of robustly flavored Mexican chocolate compounded with coarse sugar, cinnamon, and darkly roasted cocoa beans, chocolate I often buy to use in hot chocolate drinks.

Unlike bittersweet chocolate, unsweetened (or bitter) chocolate is almost entirely composed of ground cocoa beans: The tiny specks of chocolate you see when you melt the chocolate with the cream are normal.

3 ounces bittersweet chocolate
2½ ounces unsweetened chocolate
2 cups heavy cream
3 tablespoons brandy
1 cup milk
¾ cup sugar
¾ teaspoon ground cinnamon
4 egg yolks
1 cup almonds, toasted

1   Melt the bittersweet and unsweetened chocolate with the heavy cream and brandy in a saucepan over low heat. Set aside.

2   Heat the milk, sugar, and cinnamon until warm. Stir together the egg yolks, then gradually add some of the warm milk to them, whisking constantly.

3   Pour the warmed egg yolks back into the saucepan and cook over low heat, stirring constantly with a wooden or heat-resistant spatula, scraping the bottom, until the custard thickens enough to coat the spatula. Strain the custard into the chocolate and cream mixture and stir them together. Chill thoroughly in the refrigerator, then freeze in an ice cream maker according to the manufacturer's instructions.

4   Coarsely chop the almonds with a chef's knife and stir them into the ice cream when you remove it from the ice cream maker.

Note: Top-quality unsweetened chocolate can be ordered from Scharffen Berger Chocolate (see Sources, page 205).

BUTTERSCOTCH ICE CREAM
WITH WILD HICKORY NUTS

ABOUT 1 QUART

This ice cream is very special to me. I was asked to make dessert for a surprise seventieth birthday party held at the Mondavi winery for Marion Cunningham, probably the only person who likes butterscotch better than I do. I folded a few handfuls of toasty wild hickory nuts into the ice cream right before it was served, as it came out of the ice cream freezer. In addition to this ice cream, there were over twenty-five different, and spectacular, cakes, all baked in Marion's honor by America's best bakers. Of course, she loved it all.

6 tablespoons granulated sugar

¾ cup dark brown sugar, firmly packed

4 tablespoons (½ stick) butter

½ cup plus 1½ cups heavy cream

¾ cup half-and-half

½ teaspoon salt

6 egg yolks

1 cup wild hickory nuts (or pecans), toasted (see Note)

1 See the caramelization guidelines on page 200. Sprinkle the sugar in an even layer into a heavy medium-size saucepan (at least 4 quarts). Heat the sugar until it begins to liquefy around the edges. As the sugar melts, gently stir it occasionally with a wooden spoon or a heat-resistant spatula to prevent it from burning in any one spot.

2 Once the sugar begins to darken in color, it will cook very quickly. When the edges begin to bubble and the amber-colored sugar has begun to smoke, remove from the heat and quickly stir in the dark brown sugar and the butter.

3 Stir in ½ cup of the heavy cream, the half-and-half, and the salt. In a separate bowl, stir together the egg yolks, then gradually add some of the butterscotch cream to them, whisking the yolks constantly as you pour in the warm cream. Pour the mixture back into the saucepan. The brown sugar is acidic, which makes the mixture look somewhat curdled at this point, but it will come together once it has been cooked and strained.

4 Cook over low to moderate heat, constantly stirring and scraping the bottom, until the custard thickens enough to coat the spatula. Strain the custard into the remaining 1½ cups of heavy cream, chill thoroughly, and then freeze in an ice cream maker according to the manufacturer's instructions. Coarsely chop the hickory nuts (or pecans) and stir them into the frozen custard when you remove it from the ice cream maker.

Note: Wild hickory nuts are seasonally available by mail order from American Spoon Foods (see Sources, page 203).

FROZEN NOUGAT

10 TO 12 SERVINGS

This is a good frozen dessert to make if you don't have a home ice cream freezer, which I didn't for many years. This recipe makes a little extra praline, so there's enough to snack on while you finish the recipe—something I can't resist doing, myself.

The praline:

⅓ cup sugar

½ cup sliced almonds, lightly toasted

The frozen nougat:

6 tablespoons honey

2 tablespoons sugar

4 egg whites, at room temperature

Pinch of salt

1 cup heavy cream

⅓ cup shelled pistachio nuts

½ teaspoon orange flower water (see Note)

1½ tablespoons chopped candied orange peel (page 166) or grated fresh orange zest

1   To make the praline: See the caramelization guidelines on page 200. Lightly oil a baking sheet with vegetable oil or almond oil. In a heavy sauté pan, spread the ⅓ cup of sugar in an even layer. Cook over medium heat until the sugar melts and begins to darken at the edges. Stir gently with a heatproof utensil to make sure all the sugar liquefies evenly.

2   Continue to cook the melted sugar until it caramelizes to a medium amber color. Remove from the heat and immediately stir in the sliced almonds, coating them with the caramel. Spread the almonds and caramel out onto the oiled baking sheet and cool. When the praline has cooled and hardened, chop into small irregular pieces with a chef's knife or in a food processor.

3   To make the nougat: Line a 2-quart loaf pan with plastic wrap, and refrigerate.

4   Heat the honey and sugar in a small saucepan fitted with a thermometer. When the syrup reaches a temperature of about 200 degrees, start beating the egg whites and the pinch of salt with an electric mixer.

5   When the whites form soft peaks and the syrup has reached 250 degrees, pour the syrup in a steady stream into the whites while continuing to beat. Pour the syrup close to the side of the mixing bowl. If you pour it onto the metal beaters, much of the syrup will be sprayed onto the sides of the mixing bowl and won't be incorporated into the whites. (A quantity of syrup this small is

easy to overheat to temperatures higher than 250 degrees. If you do, add a few tablespoons of water to cool it down, and cook until the temperature again reads 250 degrees.)

6   Continue to beat the meringue until it cools to room temperature, about 5 minutes. Whip the cream in a separate bowl until it is mounding but still quite soft. While the cream is whipping, coarsely chop the pistachios. Fold the whipped cream into the nougat base along with the orange flower water, pistachios, candied peel or grated zest, and chopped praline. Transfer the nougat into the prepared loaf pan. Tap the pan a few times on the countertop to remove any air pockets. Cover the loaf pan tightly with plastic wrap and freeze for at least 8 hours or until firm. (The nougat can also be frozen in an unlined plastic or metal container and scooped out for serving.)

7   To serve, remove the loaf pan from the freezer. Uncover it, briefly dip the bottom of the pan in warm water, and unmold the nougat onto a platter. Peel off the plastic wrap and slice the nougat with a sharp knife dipped in hot water. Serve each piece with sliced ripe figs and fresh pears, or sliced poached pears (page 82) with some of their poaching liquid reduced to a syrupy consistency.

Note: Orange flower water, an important flavor in nougat, is sold in Middle Eastern markets, liquor stores, and supermarkets.

CHAMPAGNE GELÉE WITH CITRUS FRUITS AND KUMQUATS

6 SERVINGS

In a tall elegant glass, colorful orange and grapefruit sections sparkle suspended in shimmering spoonfuls of utterly refreshing clear gelée, garnished with thin strips of candied peel.

For a truly special event like New Year's Eve, consider stopping by your art supply store and buying a little packet of edible gold leaf.

The Champagne gelée:
½ cup plus ½ cup water
2 envelopes powdered gelatin
1 cup sugar
1 bottle (750 ml) good-quality Champagne, Prosecco, or Asti sparkling wine
Juice of ½ lime

The citrus fruits and assembly:
2 tablespoons sugar
½ cup water
12 kumquats, rinsed
3 pink grapefruits
4 navel or blood oranges
Soft candied citrus peel (page 197)
Optional: Gold leaf

1   To make the Champagne gelée: Pour ½ cup of the water into a large bowl. Sprinkle the gelatin over the water and allow it to soften for 5 minutes.

2   Heat the remaining ½ cup of water with the sugar until the sugar is dissolved.

3   After the gelatin has soaked for 5 minutes, pour the hot water and sugar over the gelatin and stir until the gelatin granules have completely dissolved. Add the Champagne, which will foam up (the reason for the large bowl I told you to use!), and lime juice. Taste and add additional lime juice if desired.

4   Cover the Champagne mixture and refrigerate until set, at least 6 hours. To speed up the jelling, first stir the gelée in an ice bath until it begins to thicken (see the instructions on page 10).

5   To prepare the fruits and assemble the gelées: Heat the sugar and the water until the sugar is dissolved. While the mixture's heating, slice the kumquats, discarding the end pieces and the seeds. Add the kumquats to the syrup and allow them to soak for 15 minutes, then drain off the syrup.

6   Peel and remove the sections and membranes from both the grapefruits and the oranges. Discard any seeds.

7 Choose six attractive stemmed glasses. Spoon some of the chilled Champagne gelée into each glass. Add a few sections of the fruits, some strips of candied peel, and a few pieces of gold leaf, if using. Spoon more of the gelée over the fruit. Continue to layer the fruits and the gelée with gold leaf and candied peel until each glass is finished. Chill until ready to serve.

CONCORD GRAPE "JELLY"

4 SERVINGS

I love the forceful flavor of Concord grapes (Vitis labrusca) in desserts. What's more, I've been told that in Asian medicine, such grapes are believed to thicken and strengthen the blood.

I often made this dish—a gelée, or chilled gelatin dessert, not jelly—at Monsoon. The strong familiar flavor of Concord grapes cuts right through the confusion in your mouth that might follow a meal of the exotic Asian flavors of sea slugs, turtle eggs, and jellyfish. I always served peanut butter cookies with the grape jelly, because the pairing of peanut butter and Concord grapes always reminds me of my childhood lunch boxes, and I hoped to awaken the same reassuring nostalgia among our customers.

2 pounds Concord grapes (or a similar variety, such as Niabell)
1 tablespoon powdered gelatin
½ cup plus ¼ cup water

¼ cup sugar
Peanut butter cookies (page 142)

1   Rinse the grapes, remove their stems, and crush them to break the skins. You can either do this by hand or in an electric mixer equipped with a dough hook running at low speed.

2   Cook the grapes over medium heat in a nonreactive pot until the skins burst and the grapes are soft and juicy, 15 to 30 minutes. In the meantime, chill four serving glasses or wine goblets.

3   Strain the grapes through a food mill or press them through a strainer. Discard the skins and the seeds. Strain the juice again, through cheesecloth or a jelly bag. You should have about 3 cups of grape juice.

4   Sprinkle the gelatin over ½ cup of the water to soften for 5 minutes. Meanwhile, make a syrup by heating the remaining ¼ cup of water with the sugar until the sugar dissolves.

5   Stir the warm (but not boiling) syrup into the gelatin and stir until the granules of gelatin are completely dissolved. Stir the warm grape juice into the gelatin mixture. Pour the grape gelatin into glasses and chill for 2 to 3 hours, until firm. To speed up the jelling, first stir the gelée in an ice bath until it begins to thicken (see the instructions on page 10). Serve with peanut butter cookies.

Variation: *You can use 3 cups of bottled Concord grape juice or any good bottled grape juice for this recipe. I recommend warming it before you add it to the gelatin.*

RED WINE GELÉE WITH PEACHES

4 TO 6 SERVINGS

A very grown-up Jell-O . . .

The red wine gelée:

¼ cup plus ¼ cup water

2 teaspoons powdered gelatin (slightly less than 1 envelope)

½ cup sugar

2 cups red wine, preferably a fruity Zinfandel or Merlot

The peaches:

2 or 3 ripe peaches (about 1 pound)

Sugar, to taste

1   To make the red wine gelée: Pour ¼ cup of water into a bowl. Sprinkle the gelatin evenly over the water and allow to soften for 5 minutes.

2   Meanwhile, make a syrup by heating the remaining ¼ cup of water with the sugar until the sugar dissolves. Stir the warm (but not boiling) syrup into the gelatin until the gelatin has completely dissolved. Check with your fingers to make sure there are no undissolved granules of gelatin.

3   Stir the wine into the gelatin mixture. Cover and refrigerate. The gelée will set in 2 to 3 hours. To speed up the jelling, first stir the gelée in an ice bath until it begins to thicken (see the instructions on page 10).

4   When ready to serve, peel the peaches, cut them into ¼-inch-thick slices, and toss with sugar to taste. Spoon the gelée into goblets and garnish with the juicy sugared peaches.

Compliments are like cookies: They're
sweet, and hard to resist. One of the
very sweetest—and I've heard it
more than once—is this: "You
make the best cookies!" These
are wonderful words, and you'll
hear them, too, if you hover
over cookies the way I do,
always trying to make sure
that each individual cookie
is perfectly baked. After all,
it is just conceivable that
someone with more
willpower than I have may
decide to have only one—so
it better be good. And that
means you've got to keep
your eye on the oven and
watch your cookies like
a hawk.

COOKIES AND CANDIES

There really is nothing better than a plate piled with excellent fresh homemade cookies—either a single kind or, better yet, an assortment, so there will be different tastes and you won't fill up on just one. I always have a few rolls of cookie dough in the freezer so they'll be there when I need them: for unexpected guests or for an impromptu batch to take along to a party.

This chapter also has a few selected candy recipes. Despite most people's expectation that candy making has to be time-consuming and difficult, these recipes are remarkably easy to make and require no special equipment. They're all on the list of things I like to have on hand so that there's something to snack on when I need a little sweetness or so that I can put together an impromptu gift candy box.

CHOCOLATE CHUNK COOKIES

ABOUT 50 COOKIES

These cookies are the ultimate crowd-pleaser, since everyone likes chocolate chip cookies, especially when they're loaded with big chunks of chocolate. I prefer to chop the chocolate myself instead of using commercial chips, which are made of chocolate that is specifically formulated not to melt.

This recipe was inspired by the excellent chocolate chip cookies Nancy Silverton makes at Campanile in Los Angeles. Chocolate chip cookies go great with almost anything, or they can make a perfect dessert by themselves, piled high on a plate. And they're not bad for breakfast, either.

2 cups nuts, toasted (walnuts, pecans, almonds, or macadamia nuts)

½ pound butter (2 sticks), at room temperature

1 cup light brown sugar, firmly packed

¾ cup granulated sugar

1 teaspoon vanilla extract

2 eggs, at room temperature

2½ cups flour

¾ teaspoon baking soda

14 ounces bittersweet chocolate, roughly chopped into ½- to 1-inch chunks (about 3 cups)

1   Coarsely chop the nuts. Cream the butter with the brown sugar, granulated sugar, and vanilla. If you use an electric mixer, it will take about 1 minute. Stop the mixer once during beating to scrape down the sides of the bowl with a rubber spatula so all the butter gets incorporated.

2   Add the eggs, one at a time, and continue beating until thoroughly mixed.

3   Mix together the flour and baking soda and stir into the creamed butter and sugar. Stir in the nuts and chocolate chunks.

4   Transfer the cookie dough to a lightly floured surface, divide it in four, and use your hands to roll each piece of dough into a log about 9 inches long. Wrap the logs in plastic wrap and refrigerate until firm, about 1 hour. The dough can also be frozen at this point for up to 2 months.

5   To bake the cookies, position the oven racks in the center and upper part of the oven. Preheat the oven to 350 degrees.

6   Slice each log into ¾-inch-thick slices and place the cookies on parchment-covered baking sheets, 3 inches apart. If any unbaked cookies fall apart, push them back together with your hands on the baking sheet. Bake for 10 minutes, rotating the baking sheets and switching racks midway through baking. When done, the cookies should be very lightly colored in the center, and just barely baked—if you like chocolate chip cookies chewy, as I do. Once they have cooled, store the cookies in an airtight container.

PEANUT BUTTER COOKIES

ABOUT 35 COOKIES

Everyone I know likes peanut butter cookies, except my friend Fritz, and he changed his mind one afternoon at my house after wolfing down an entire plateful of these exceptionally peanut-buttery ones. I like them with my coffee in the afternoon. Inspired by childhood lunch-box memories, at Monsoon I offered a whimsical dessert of peanut butter cookies served with Concord grape "jelly" (page 132).

4 tablespoons (½ stick) butter, at room temperature

½ cup granulated sugar

½ cup light brown sugar, firmly packed

1 cup creamy peanut butter

1 egg, at room temperature

1¼ cups flour

¼ teaspoon salt

1 tablespoon baking powder

1   Position the oven racks in the center and upper part of the oven and preheat the oven to 350 degrees.

2   Beat together the butter, sugars, and peanut butter. In a standing electric mixer this will take 2 minutes at medium speed. Stop the mixer once to scrape down the sides of the bowl to make sure that the butter is completely incorporated. Beat in the egg.

3   In a separate bowl, stir together the flour, salt, and baking powder.

4   Mix the dry ingredients into the creamed butter and peanut butter until the dough starts to come together.

5   Roll the dough into 1-inch balls (the dough will be crumbly, so press the balls in the palm of your hand), roll them in sugar, and place them 3 inches apart on parchment-lined baking sheets. When you've filled one baking sheet, mark the tops of the cookies with a fork, crisscrossing and pressing down slightly twice.

6   Bake for 9 minutes, until the cookies begin to brown along the edges. I remove them from the oven at this point, before I think they are done, since I like my peanut butter cookies soft and chewy. Once they have cooled, store the cookies in an airtight container.

Note: You can make this dough several days before baking. Or roll the dough into 1-inch balls and freeze for up to 2 months.

FLO'S CHOCOLATE SNAPS

ABOUT 70 COOKIES

A snappy chocolate cookie from my friend Flo Braker. Unusually flavorful for a butter cookie, and with a short crispness that explodes with chocolate flavor in your mouth. I also use these to make ice cream sandwiches— simply roll the dough into larger-size logs or, if you are a traditionalist, roll out the dough with a rolling pin on a lightly floured surface, cut the snap dough into rectangles, bake them, and then use them for ice cream sandwiches.

½ pound (2 sticks) butter, at room temperature

1¼ cups sugar, plus more for sprinkling on the cookies

½ teaspoon vanilla extract

1 egg, at room temperature

1 egg yolk, at room temperature

¾ cup cocoa (preferably Dutch-processed)

3 cups flour

2½ teaspoons baking powder

¼ teaspoon salt

1   Beat together the butter and the 1¼ cups of sugar until smooth, about 1 minute in an electric mixer. Stop the mixer and scrape down the sides to make sure all the butter is incorporated. Do not overbeat. Add the vanilla.

2   Beat in the egg and the egg yolk, stopping again to scrape the sides of the mixing bowl.

3   Sift together the cocoa, flour, baking powder, and salt. Set the mixer at the lowest speed and gradually add the dry ingredients, mixing until completely incorporated. There should be no streaks of butter visible.

4   Divide the dough into three pieces. On a lightly floured surface, roll each portion with your hands into a log about 7 inches long and 2 inches in diameter. Wrap the logs in plastic and refrigerate them until they're firm enough to slice. The dough can also be frozen at this point for up to 2 months.

5   To bake the snaps, position the oven racks in the center and upper part of the oven, and preheat the oven to 350 degrees. Slice the logs into ⅓-inch-thick rounds and bake on parchment-lined baking sheets for 10 to 12 minutes, until puffed and slightly firm. Rotate the baking sheets and switch racks midway through baking to make sure the cookies bake evenly. Remove the cookies from the oven and sprinkle the warm cookies with sugar. Allow to cool completely. They will continue to firm up and get "snappy" as they cool. Once they have cooled, store the cookies in an airtight container.

GINGERSNAPS

Use the freshest spices you can get for these gingersnaps. Once when I was in a bind, I used some cinnamon that was years—possibly decades—old, and the results were terrible: no spicy zing!

½ pound (2 sticks) butter, at room temperature

1¼ cups granulated sugar

¼ cup molasses

1 teaspoon vanilla extract

2 eggs

3 cups flour

2½ teaspoons baking soda

½ teaspoon salt

2½ teaspoons ground cinnamon

2 teaspoons ground ginger

1½ teaspoons ground black pepper

½ teaspoon ground cloves

Optional: ¼ cup finely chopped candied ginger (page 165) or candied lemon peel (page 166)

Coarse sugar or granulated sugar

1   Beat together the butter and sugar. This will take about 1 minute in a standing electric mixer. Stop the mixer during beating and scrape the sides of the bowl to make sure the butter is completely incorporated. Stir in the molasses and vanilla.

2   Stir in the eggs, one at a time, until thoroughly incorporated.

3   Sift together the flour, baking soda, salt, and all the spices (cinnamon, ginger, pepper, and cloves).

4   Mix the dry ingredients into the creamed butter mixture until they are thoroughly incorporated and there are no streaks of butter in the dough. Mix in the optional candied ginger or candied peel.

5   Divide the dough in four. On a lightly floured surface, with your hands roll each portion into a log about 8 inches long and 1½ inches in diameter. Wrap the logs in plastic and refrigerate them until they're firm enough to slice. The dough can also be frozen at this point for up to 2 months.

6   When you're ready to bake the gingersnaps, position the oven racks in the center and upper part of the oven and preheat the oven to 350 degrees.

7   Cut the chilled dough into round ½-inch-thick slices. Dip one side of each slice in granulated sugar, and place the cookies, sugared sides up and about 3 inches apart, on baking sheets lined with parchment paper.

8   Bake for about 10 minutes. For even baking, rotate the baking sheets and switch racks about midway through baking. When uniformly browned, take them out of the oven. Once they have cooled, store the cookies in an airtight container.

Note: Coarse or crystal sugar gives gingersnaps a truly crispy crunch when you bite into them. The coarse sugar I use is Hawaiian washed raw sugar, available in most supermarkets. Crystal sugar is available at baking supply stores and from Sweet Celebrations (see Sources, page 205).

POPPY SEED–ORANGE COOKIES

ABOUT 18 SANDWICH COOKIES

These buttery shortbread cookies have an exciting poppy seed crunch. Inspired by my obligatory breakfast bagel, I started making little poppy seed shortbread cookie sandwiches filled with homemade jam. You can use whatever kind of jam you like, homemade or store-bought, and you should feel free to experiment with different shapes, too: rectangles or triangles or, on St. Valentine's Day, hearts.

½ pound (2 sticks) butter, at room temperature

½ cup sugar

1 egg yolk, at room temperature

Zest of 2 oranges or lemons, finely chopped or grated, or ⅓ cup finely chopped candied peel (page 197)

½ teaspoon vanilla extract

2 teaspoons orange liqueur

2 cups flour

6 tablespoons poppy seeds

About ½ cup strained jam

1   Beat together the butter and sugar until completely combined, about 1 minute with an electric mixer. Stir in the egg yolk, the citrus zest or candied peel, vanilla, and orange liqueur.

2   Stir in the flour and poppy seeds and mix until the dough comes together in a single mass. Wrap the dough in plastic wrap and form into a rectangle about 1 inch thick. Refrigerate the dough for 1 hour.

3   To bake, position the oven racks in the center and upper parts of the oven and preheat the oven to 350 degrees.

4   Divide the dough into two pieces. On a lightly floured surface, roll out the dough about ½ inch thick. If necessary, sprinkle the surface with more flour to prevent the dough from sticking. Brush off any excess flour from the dough.

5   Use a 2-inch round cookie cutter to cut out circles of the cookie dough. Place them on a parchment-lined baking sheet, spaced 1 inch apart. Roll out the other piece of dough, cut out the same number of cookies, and cut a small hole in the center of each one with a round ½-inch piping tip. Gather up scraps of dough left behind, roll out again, and cut out additional circles, half with holes, half without.

6   Bake for about 12 minutes, until the sides of the cookies turn a pale light brown. Midway through baking, rotate the baking sheets and switch racks. Remove from oven and cool completely before filling.

7   Spread 1 rounded teaspoon of jam on the flat bottom side of the cookies without holes in them. Top them with the cookies with holes, bottom side down, making jam sandwiches. Store the cookies in an airtight container.

Variations: *For a more exotic taste, substitute ¼ to ½ teaspoon of orange flower water for the orange liqueur.*

You can also make a chocolate ganache filling for the cookies by heating 2 ounces of chopped bittersweet chocolate with 3 tablespoons of heavy cream, stirring until the chocolate melts. Use 1 teaspoon of the chocolate filling for each cookie sandwich. Ganache-filled cookies should be stored in the refrigerator and allowed to come to room temperature before serving.

FIG COOKIES

ABOUT 30 COOKIES

This is a close adaptation of a recipe from the Downtown Bakery & Creamery in Healdsburg, California, run by my friend Kathleen Stewart. Kathleen was a waitress at Chez Panisse for many years before moving to a small town in Sonoma County and becoming one of the area's finest bakers. Each time I visit the bakery, I find something wonderful to try.

One San Francisco society matron liked the bakery so much, she got in the habit of taking a taxicab all the way to Healdsburg (about ninety miles north of the city), where she would march into the bakery, hand the counterperson an enormous wad of twenties, and say, "Fill up as many boxes as you can for that, please." I exhibit a little more restraint, and usually buy several sticky buns, some almond tarts, and a few fig cookies.

The fig filling:
2 cups halved dried figs
1/3 cup granulated sugar
Grated zest of 1 lemon
1/4 teaspoon vanilla extract

The dough:
6 tablespoons (3/4 stick) butter, at room temperature

2/3 cup light brown sugar
1/2 teaspoon vanilla extract
2 eggs, at room temperature
2 1/2 cups flour
1/2 teaspoon baking powder
1/4 teaspoon ground cinnamon
1/2 teaspoon salt

1   To make the fig filling: Trim off and discard the hard stems of the figs. Put the figs in a saucepan with the sugar and lemon zest, cover with water, and bring to the boil. Reduce the heat and simmer the figs for 30 minutes, until tender. Add more boiling water during cooking if water evaporates and the figs are no longer covered.

2   When the figs are tender, remove them from the saucepan with a slotted spoon and pass them through a food mill or purée them in a food processor. Stir in the 1/4 teaspoon vanilla, and set the filling aside to cool while you make the dough.

3   To make the cookie dough: Beat together the butter and the brown sugar until smooth, about 1 minute if you're using an electric mixer. Add the vanilla, then the eggs, one at a time. If you're using an electric mixer, stop and scrape down the sides of the bowl. Continue beating until the eggs are completely incorporated.

4   In a separate bowl, mix together the flour, baking powder, cinnamon, and salt. Gradually stir the dry ingredients into the creamed butter mixture until the dough comes together.

5   Gather up the dough and divide it into four pieces. Shape each piece into a rectangle roughly 3/4 inch thick, wrap the pieces of dough in plastic, and refrigerate for at least 30 minutes.

6   To assemble and bake the fig cookies, first position two oven racks in the center and upper part of the oven. Preheat the oven to 350 degrees.

7   On a lightly floured surface, roll out the first piece of dough into a rectangle about 5 by 9 inches. Spread one quarter of the fig filling evenly in a lengthwise strip down the center of the dough, keeping the fig purée piled up a bit in the center. Run a long metal spatula underneath the dough to make sure that it is not sticking to your rolling area.

8   Brush all the exposed surfaces of the dough lightly with water. Fold the dough around the fig filling as if you were folding a letter: Fold the long top edge of the dough toward you to cover at least half the filling, then fold the bottom edge up over the rest of the filling, overlapping the top edge a little and completely encasing the filling.

9   Line two baking sheets with parchment and place the cookie roll on one of them, seam side down. Pinch the ends of the roll together to completely enclose the filling. Repeat the process with the three remaining pieces of dough and the rest of the filling, putting two cookie rolls on each baking sheet.

10   Bake for 20 to 25 minutes, until the dough is a deep golden brown. Rotate the baking sheets and switch racks midway through baking.

11   Remove the cookie rolls from the oven and cool for at least 15 minutes. With a sharp serrated knife, slice the rolls into 1-inch-thick cookies, either diagonally or straight across. Once they have cooled completely, store the cookies in an airtight container.

Serving suggestion: *Serve fig cookies with mint tea or with the mint sherbet on page 116.*

MEXICAN WEDDING COOKIES

ABOUT 50 COOKIES

My multitalented Chez Panisse colleague and friend Stephanie Sugawara used to make these for everyone on the staff. When Linda Zagula, another pastry department coworker, got married, she declined our offer to bake her an elaborate wedding cake. Instead she asked Stephanie to bake her a giant platter of these cookies. Linda wanted there to be more than enough for everybody, especially herself.

½ pound (2 sticks) butter, at room temperature

⅓ cup granulated sugar

1 teaspoon vanilla extract

1 cup pecans, toasted

2¼ cups flour

1 teaspoon water

Powdered sugar for dredging the cookies

1   Beat together the butter, sugar, and vanilla until smooth. If using an electric mixer, this will take about 1 minute. Stop the mixer during beating and scrape the sides of the mixing bowl to make sure the butter is completely incorporated. Chop the pecans very fine.

2   Stir half the flour into the creamed butter, then add the water.

3   Mix in the remaining flour and the chopped pecans. Chill the cookie dough until it's firm enough to handle, about 1 hour.

4   Position the oven racks in the center and upper part of the oven and preheat the oven to 350 degrees.

5   Use your hands to roll the cookie dough into 1-inch balls and place them on parchment-lined baking sheets.

6   Bake the cookies for 15 minutes. For even baking, rotate the baking sheets and switch racks midway through baking. Remove from the oven and cool.

7   Sift some powdered sugar into a bowl. Toss the cookies in the sugar, five at a time, until they are completely coated with a thick layer. Because there is relatively little sugar in these cookies, be generous when coating them. Store the cookies in an airtight container.

PECAN TUILES

TWELVE 5-INCH COOKIES

Tuiles (French for "tiles") are crispy cookies bent—while still warm and bendable—into the shape of terra-cotta roof tiles. This recipe doesn't completely reinvent the tuile, but it is a little easier to make than the more familiar almond tuile formula because the cookies don't need to be painstakingly spread out onto the baking sheet with a spatula. Instead the cookies spread to their final dimensions as they bake. The warm cookies can be draped over a rolling pin (to make roof tile shapes) or overturned custard cups (to make cookie cups); or they can be rolled around the handle of a wooden spoon (to make tubes).

4 tablespoons (½ stick) butter

¼ cup light brown sugar, firmly packed

¼ cup light corn syrup

¼ cup pecans, lightly toasted

6 tablespoons flour

1   Position the oven rack in the center of the oven. Preheat the oven to 400 degrees.

2   Melt together the butter, brown sugar, and corn syrup over low heat. Chop the pecans very fine.

3   Stir the pecans and the flour into the melted butter mixture.

4   Line an unwarped baking sheet with parchment paper. For shaping the baked tuiles, have a rolling pin ready, placed on a folded dish towel to steady it. It's easiest to bake the cookies one baking sheet at a time, 4 cookies to the sheet, allowing 1 table-spoon of batter per cookie. Put four spoonfuls on the baking sheet, spaced equally apart, and flatten them slightly with damp fingers.

5   Bake for about 7 minutes. For even baking, rotate the baking sheet midway through baking. When done, they will be a deep golden brown.

6   Remove from the oven and cool briefly, about 1 minute. Using a metal spatula, lift each tuile off the baking sheet and drape over the rolling pin to form the tuiles. As the cookies cool, they harden and become brittle. If they cool too quickly, before you have time to shape them, they can be softened by putting them back in the oven for 1 minute.

7   Allow the pan to cool, then continue baking additional tuiles.

8   Store the cooled tuiles in an airtight container until ready to serve. These are best eaten within a few hours of baking.

SESAME ORANGE ALMOND TUILES

ABOUT 20 COOKIES

This is another tuile recipe with a very distinct personality. Like the pecan tuiles, they can also be shaped into cookie cups or tubes or cones. They make delightfully unusual ice cream cones—especially for the white chocolate–ginger ice cream on page 122.

3 tablespoons butter, melted

1 tablespoon sesame oil

3 tablespoons orange juice

Grated zest of 1 orange

10 tablespoons sugar

¼ cup flour

¾ cup sliced almonds

2 tablespoons white sesame seeds

½ tablespoon black sesame seeds

1   Mix together the butter, sesame oil, orange juice, orange zest, and sugar.

2   Stir in the flour, almonds, and white and black sesame seeds. Let the batter rest for 1 hour at room temperature.

3   Position the oven rack in the center of the oven. Preheat the oven to 375 degrees.

4   Place a rolling pin on a folded dish towel to steady it. Bake the tuiles on an unwarped, parchment-lined baking sheet, 6 tuiles to the sheet, allowing 1 tablespoon of the batter for each cookie. Bake the tuiles for 8 to 9 minutes, rotating the baking sheet midway through baking.

5   When they are just browned, all the way through to the center, remove them from the oven. When they are just cool enough to handle but still pliable, lift them, one at a time—working quickly—and drape each one over the rolling pin. If some of the tuiles cool down too much and do not bend easily, leave them on the baking sheet and return them to the oven for 30 to 45 seconds to rewarm them. When the tuiles have all cooled, store them in an airtight container, but serve within a few hours of baking.

AMARETTI COOKIES

ABOUT 60 COOKIES

To me, crumbled crunchy amaretti make desserts taste Italian. This may be because amaretti conjure up memories of bakeries in Italian neighborhoods like North Beach in San Francisco, where it seems as if every multilayered, syrup-soaked sponge cake temptation incorporates these crispy, not-too-sweet macaroons.

If you can get them, 6 or 7 bitter almonds pulverized with the almonds can replace the almond extract, making these macaroons perhaps worthier of their name: amaretti *is Italian for "little bitter ones." The amaretti and amarettini di Saronno that are widely available, in colorful tins, individually wrapped in prettily printed tissue paper, are indeed imported from Saronno, Italy, but they differ from these in being made not with almonds but with the bitter almondlike kernels of apricot pits.*

1 cup almonds, toasted
1 teaspoon flour
½ cup powdered sugar
2 egg whites, at room temperature

Pinch of cream of tartar
6 tablespoons granulated sugar
1 teaspoon almond extract

1   Position the oven rack in the center of the oven. Preheat the oven to 300 degrees.

2   Pulverize the almonds in a food processor with the flour and powdered sugar.

3   Whisk the egg whites until they become frothy. Add the cream of tartar and continue whisking, increasing your speed, until they begin to hold their shape. Gradually whisk in the granulated sugar and beat until they form soft, rounded peaks.

4   Fold the ground nut mixture and almond extract into the beaten whites with a rubber spatula.

5   Onto a parchment-lined baking sheet, using a pastry bag fitted with a large plain ½-inch tip, pipe out the cookies in mounds about 1½ inches in diameter and about ¾ inch apart. Bake for 35 minutes, until the macaroons have browned. Turn off the oven, leaving the cookies in it to dry out for an additional 20 minutes.

6   Remove the amaretti from the oven and cool completely. Stored in an airtight container, they will keep for several weeks.

ALMOND CHOCOLATE BISCOTTI

ABOUT 60 COOKIES

A strong contender for the perfect cookie. These biscotti are easy to make and they keep for at least a week. Whenever I made these at the restaurants I worked in, I was certain that the staff ate more of them than the customers did—but no one ever confessed.

Although this recipe makes a lot of cookies, you may be surprised at how quickly they disappear from your kitchen, too. The combination of big chunks of chocolate and toasted almonds in crispy biscotti is irresistible.

3 eggs
1 cup sugar
½ teaspoon vanilla extract
1¼ cups almonds, toasted
2½ cups flour

1 teaspoon baking powder
7 ounces bittersweet chocolate, roughly chopped into ½- to 1-inch chunks (about 1½ cups)

1   Position the oven rack in the center of the oven. Preheat the oven to 350 degrees.

2   Using an electric mixer with a whip attachment or a whisk, whip the eggs, sugar, and vanilla until the mixture thickens and holds its shape when you lift the whisk.

3   Coarsely chop the almonds.

4   Sift together the flour and the baking powder and mix into the egg mixture. Stir in the nuts and chocolate.

5   Line a baking sheet with parchment paper. Form the dough into two logs on the sheet, each log about 3 inches wide and almost as long as the baking sheet. Dampen your hands and smooth each log.

6   Bake for 25 minutes, until light brown. When done, remove the baking sheet from the oven and turn the temperature down to 300 degrees. Let the biscotti logs cool for a few minutes.

7   Remove the baked biscotti logs from the pan and peel off the parchment paper. With a long serrated knife, slice the logs diagonally into ½-inch-thick slices.

8   Place the sliced cookies flat on two baking sheets and bake for an additional 20 minutes. The cookies should be golden brown when done. Cool and store in an airtight container for up to a week.

CHOCOLATE ALMOND NUT JOBS

20 TO 30 CANDIES

These candies are named after me, because whenever I made them, Mary Jo, another pastry cook, would say, "Dave, you're a nut job!" Soon everyone in the pastry department was calling them "Dave's nut jobs"—affectionately, I hope. These are just about the easiest candies you can make, and among the best, as long as you use very good nuts, perfectly toasted, and equally good chocolate.

¾ **cup almonds**   **4 ounces bittersweet chocolate**

1   Preheat the oven to 350 degrees. Toast the almonds in the oven for 8 to 10 minutes, until they are lightly browned. Allow them to cool completely, and then chop them coarsely.

2   Break up the chocolate and melt it in a bowl set over a pan of simmering water. Make sure that the bowl you melt the chocolate in is completely dry; if there's even a drop of water, the chocolate will "seize"—become stiff and granular—and it will be unusable.

3   Once the chocolate has melted, take the bowl off the heat and stir in the chopped nuts, completely coating them with chocolate.

4   Cover a baking sheet with parchment or plastic wrap. Scoop out heaping tablespoons of the chocolate-nut mixture onto the sheet pan. When done, refrigerate until ready to eat.

Variations: *You can make any kind of chocolate nut jobs: toasted pecans or walnuts are especially good. Or make them with any combination of toasted nuts. Once I made them with Rice Krispies instead of nuts! For a more formal presentation—if you want to include them in a candy box, for example—spoon the chocolate-coated nuts directly into candy cups.*

Note: By refrigerating the candies and serving them cold, you avoid having to temper the chocolate. Candies made with untempered chocolate and left at room temperature eventually develop white streaks from the gradual separation of the cocoa butter out of the chocolate.

PANFORTE

This is my version of the classic holiday confection from Siena, Italy. Lee Ann, a waitress and friend at Chez Panisse, once brought me back an assortment of panfortes when she returned from a winter vacation there. There were so many kinds I was almost overwhelmed. But I had gotten hooked on panforte, and there was no going back: I figured out what qualities I liked best in each of the examples Lee Ann had brought me, and I came up with my own recipe.

I like my panforte quite spicy (in Siena they call highly spiced panforte panpepato), so I add a brisk amount of black pepper. This makes it ideal for after dinner: sweet, but not too sweet, with a spicy bite to it. Panforte can be made well in advance and kept on hand for serving after dinner, sliced into small wedges, with strong coffee, or with vin santo. I must

5 tablespoons cocoa, plus 2 teaspoons more for dusting the pan

3 ounces bittersweet chocolate

1 cup hazelnuts, toasted, loose skins removed

1½ cups almonds, toasted

¾ cup flour

¾ cup chopped candied citrus peel (preferably candied citron, page 167)

1 tablespoon ground cinnamon

2 teaspoons ground ginger

1½ teaspoons freshly ground black pepper

Pinch of grated nutmeg

Pinch of chili pepper

1 cup granulated sugar

¾ cup honey

Powdered sugar for dusting the panforte

1   Position the oven rack in the center of the oven and preheat the oven to 300 degrees. Butter a 9½-inch springform pan. Dust the pan with the 2 teaspoons of cocoa and tap out any excess.

2   Chop the chocolate and melt it in a dry bowl set over simmering water.

3   Very coarsely chop the hazelnuts and the almonds, leaving a few whole.

4   In a large mixing bowl, stir together the hazelnuts, almonds, flour, the 5 tablespoons of cocoa, candied citrus, and spices.

5   In a small heavy saucepan fitted with a candy thermometer, mix the sugar and the honey and heat to 240 degrees.

6   Stir the chocolate into the chopped nut mixture. Stir in the honey syrup. At this point the batter will begin to stiffen, so you need to work rapidly. Transfer the batter to the prepared pan. Dampen your hand, or the back of a spoon, and use it to spread the batter evenly and smooth the surface of the panforte.

7   Bake for 50 minutes. Remove from the oven and let stand about 30 minutes. While the panforte is still warm, loosen the edges from the pan with a knife. Remove the springform and remove the bottom from the panforte with the help of a metal spatula. Cool completely.

confess, however, that occasionally when I'm searching for something else in my pantry, I come across a well-wrapped and almost forgotten disk of panforte, and I can't resist slicing off a piece, no matter what hour of the day it is.

8   Sprinkle the top of the panforte with powdered sugar and rub it in with your hands. Do the same to the bottom and the sides. Wrap the panforte tightly in plastic and store in a cool, dry place until ready to serve. It will keep for a year, and improves with age.

Note: Traditionally, panforte is baked in a pan lined with a disk of edible rice paper, which makes it much easier to remove the panforte from the pan. Edible rice paper is available by mail order from Sweet Celebrations (see Sources, page 205).

HONEY NOUGAT

ABOUT 60 CANDIES

This nougat has an elusive orange flower water flavor—and plenty of nuts. I buy pistachio nuts in small quantities, so they are crisp and fresh, and I don't toast them, so they retain that lovely brilliant green color. I have fond memories of my grandfather, who was Syrian, giving me huge ten-pound sacks of red-dyed, unshelled pistachios to snack on when I was a little boy. I ate them so fast, they only lasted a few days, at most. The red dye on my fingers, however, lasted considerably longer.

1 cup honey
3 tablespoons light corn syrup
¾ cup heavy cream
¾ cup whole almonds, toasted
¾ cup shelled pistachios

¾ cup sliced almonds, toasted
2 tablespoons finely chopped candied orange or tangerine peel (page 197)
A few drops orange flower water

1   Lightly grease a baking sheet with almond oil, or a neutral-tasting oil.

2   Measure the honey, corn syrup, and heavy cream into a heavy 4-quart saucepan, and cook, monitoring the temperature with a candy thermometer, until it reaches 265 degrees.

3   Remove from the heat and quickly stir in the nuts, citrus peel, and orange flower water. Spread the hot nougat evenly onto the greased cookie sheet and cool completely before slicing.

4   Cut into 1-inch squares with a large chef's knife brushed with a small amount of oil. Store in an airtight container.

CANDIED CITRON

ABOUT 2 CUPS

The citron is one of the oldest members of the citrus family, and all but useless as a raw fruit. However, its candied peel is an indispensable ingredient of panforte and the other desserts to which it lends its unmistakable, deliciously haunting fragrance. If you are fortunate enough to live in an area where citrons are available (usually in the winter), by all means buy some and candy the peel. What little flesh and juice there are inside are usually discarded.

The most common variety is the Etrog citron, which looks like a large, knobby lemon. Another variety, the Buddha's Hand citron, is undoubtedly the most bizarre-looking fruit there is. At the stem end it resembles an ordinary citrus fruit, but at the other it forms a tangle of elongated pointy yellow fingers that reach out in several directions.

2 citrons

3 cups sugar, plus 1 cup for tossing

2 cups water

1 tablespoon light corn syrup

1   Wash the citrons and slice them into quarters. Remove any pulp with a spoon and discard it.

2   Cut the citron rind into ½-inch cubes. Put the pieces of citron in a medium-size heavy saucepan and cover with an ample amount of water. Simmer the diced citron for 30 to 40 minutes, until translucent.

3   Drain the citron, discarding the liquid. Measure the 3 cups sugar, 2 cups water, and the corn syrup into the saucepan. Heat until the sugar is dissolved.

4   Return the citron to the syrup in the pan, attach a candy thermometer to the side, and continue cooking until the temperature reaches 230 degrees. Remove from the heat and let stand 1 hour.

5   In a strainer, drain the syrup from the citron. Allow the citron to drain for 1 hour.

6   On a baking sheet or in a bowl, toss the drained citron in the remaining 1 cup of sugar. Toss with your fingers to separate the pieces and coat them all with sugar. Spread the candied citron out on a platter or a sheet pan to dry overnight. Shake off any excess sugar and store the candied citron in an airtight container in the refrigerator for up to a year.

SUGARED KUMQUATS

ABOUT 20 KUMQUATS

These candied fruits resemble bejeweled baubles with the shape of slightly deflated footballs. First-timers are often skeptical of eating a whole fruit, peel, seeds, and all—the proper way to enjoy kumquats—and then are slightly taken aback by their assertive tang. Fresh or sugared, they are best enjoyed by popping the entire fruit into your mouth so you get the combination of the sweet texture of the flesh as you first bite into it, and then the squirt of the tart pulp and juice within. The seeds are edible, too.

½ pound (about 20) firm kumquats

1½ cups water

2 cups sugar, plus more for tossing

1   Wash the kumquats and prick each one four or five times in different places with a pin. Put them in a saucepan, cover with water, and heat to a simmer. Cook for 5 minutes, then drain.

2   In a heavy saucepan with a candy thermometer attached, heat the water and sugar, add the kumquats, and cook until they reach a temperature of 200 degrees. Let them stand in the syrup at for least 4 hours, or overnight.

3   Reheat the kumquats in the syrup until they reach 220 degrees and drain. Set the kumquats on a cooling rack to dry for several hours, then toss each one in sugar, shake off the excess, and set on the cooling rack until ready to serve.

Note: Sugared kumquats are best served within a couple of days. You may need to recoat them in sugar if the weather has been especially damp.

QUINCE PASTE

Lately it seems to me I've been seeing quince paste everywhere—in Middle Eastern markets, in Latino groceries, and in fancy restaurants. I make it at home using a big 14-inch nonstick skillet. It takes at least half an hour of constant stirring. I always wear an oven mitt when stirring it with the wooden spatula, since as the hot paste thickens it occasionally pops and sputters.

4 medium quinces (1½ pounds)
4 cups water
½ lemon

3 cups sugar, plus more for tossing

1   Wash and rub the quinces to remove any fuzz and leaves. Cut the whole fruits into 1-inch-thick chunks. Cook in the water with the lemon half over medium heat, covered, until the quince pieces are tender, about 1 hour.

2   Remove the lemon and pass the quinces through a food mill or press them through a sieve. You should have 3 to 4 cups of purée. Put the quince purée and the 3 cups sugar in a heavy non-reactive skillet.

3   Cook over low heat, stirring constantly, until the mixture forms a solid mass, about 30 to 40 minutes. It will be thick and shiny, and the bubbles will become quite large. You can test the paste for doneness by chilling a small amount in the freezer and checking it after a few minutes. It should appear jelled when you push it.

4   Spread the paste ½ inch thick onto a baking sheet that has been lined with parchment paper or very lightly oiled. When it has cooled enough to touch, wet your hand and smooth the paste again. If you find that it is not cooked enough, place the baking sheet in a very low oven (warmed briefly, then turned off) for several hours to dry it slightly. Cool completely. Store quince paste, uncovered, in a cool, dry place. Do not store it in a tightly sealed container or it will become soggy.

5   To serve, cut the paste into 1-inch squares using a sharp knife dipped in hot water. Toss the squares in sugar, shaking off excess.

Serving suggestion: *Slices of quince paste are delicious with a dry sharp cheese such as Manchego, a popular Spanish dessert combination.*

Variation: *You can also make apple paste by substituting for the quinces 3 large apples (about 2 pounds). Cook in 1 cup of water until soft, then cook down to a paste with 2 cups of sugar and a small piece of vanilla bean. I like to use Rome Beauty apples, which taste good and cook to a brilliant red color.*

The need for preserving fruit at home occurs naturally to me whenever I go to the market and see the bins overflowing with seasonal fruits at their peak, knowing that unless I do something, too many months will pass before I taste their like again. Inevitably I get a bit obsessive and end up with too many jars of preserves, and I have to give most of them away. Not that there's anything wrong with that. On the contrary, a jar of homemade Seville orange marmalade is my idea of a perfect gift for just about any occasion.

Apparently what comes naturally to me is thought to be such a fringe pursuit for most home cooks that even encyclopedic cooking references such as *Joy of Cooking* now omit preserves altogether. I love making preserves, but there isn't enough room for all my recipes in this book, so I've included a few favorites in hopes that the reader will try making them and decide that it's worthwhile and relatively easy to do, after all.

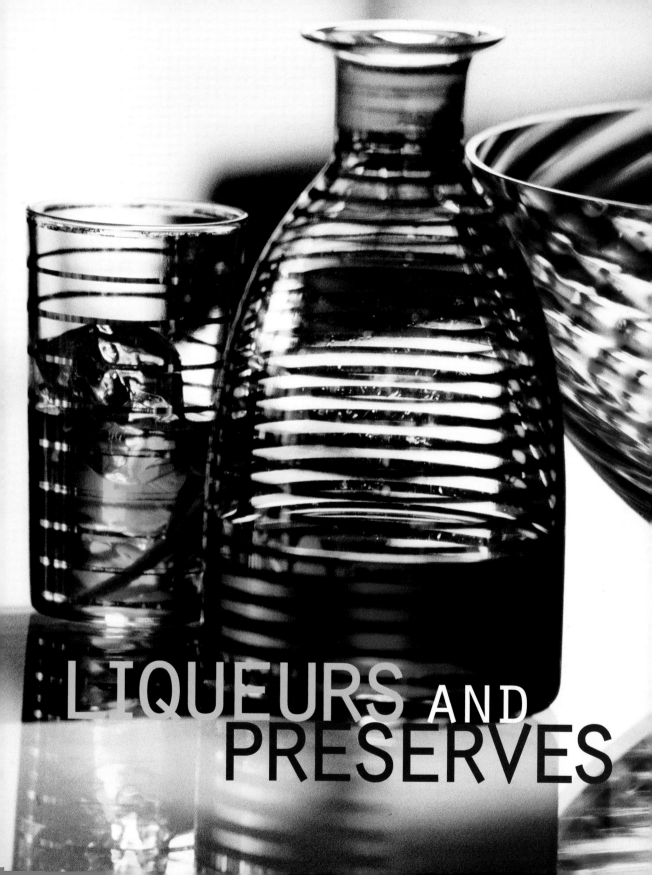

LIQUEURS AND PRESERVES

I'm seasonally inclined to make and give away bottles of liqueurs. I have a little niche in my basement where there are always a few bottles of homemade liqueurs and apéritifs. I've included two of my favorite recipes, the green walnut elixir called nocino and vin d'orange, or orange wine. Actually, only the nocino is a true liqueur, or cordial—a flavored, sweetened high-proof alcoholic beverage. My other standby gift beverage, vin d'orange, is more properly called a fortified wine—in this case, white wine, fortified with vodka, sweetened, and flavored with sour orange.

VIN D'ORANGE

ABOUT 1½ QUARTS

I often serve small glasses of vin d'orange as an apéritif. Anyone who enjoys Lillet is also likely to enjoy this fruity, slightly bitter fortified wine. But be careful—it's quite potent. Serve it over ice with a twist of orange or lemon zest. Use an inexpensive but good-tasting white wine.

Whenever I find Seville oranges at the produce market I triple or quadruple this recipe. Then I have plenty of bottles on hand to take to friends as gifts when I'm invited for dinner.

3 Seville or sour oranges
1 lemon
²/₃ cup sugar

5 cups (about 1¼ bottles) white wine
1 cup vodka
One 1-inch piece vanilla bean

1   Rinse the oranges and lemon and cut them in half.

2   In a large glass (or other nonreactive) container, mix together the sugar, white wine, and vodka until the sugar is dissolved. Add the vanilla bean and orange and lemon halves. Cover and let stand undisturbed for 1 month in a cool dark place.

3   After 1 month, remove and discard the oranges and lemon and the vanilla bean. Filter the vin d'orange through cheesecloth and pour into clean bottles. Cork tightly and keep in a cool place until ready to serve. Vin d'orange will keep for a year.

Variation: *Try using a fruity red wine instead of white. You can also use sweet oranges, but only sour oranges such as Sevilles will yield that distinctively pleasant bitterness.*

NOCINO

ABOUT 1 QUART

If you're lucky enough to have a friend with a walnut tree, or otherwise can get hold of some green, underripe walnuts, you can make nocino, a dark, slightly bitter Italian liqueur that tastes strongly of walnuts, with a hint of spice. I use it to flavor custards or to spoon over vanilla ice cream (page 121).

In Italy, the walnuts are traditionally picked on the feast of San Giovanni—midsummer's day, the twenty-fourth of June. Unfortunately, I usually forget to pick them then and a few weeks later I have to make a mad dash up to my friend Kathleen Stewart's walnut tree at her house in Sonoma County, just before the shells of the ripening walnuts have gotten too firm. Be careful quartering the green walnuts; their husks can be very hard and may resist all but the most forceful and persistent knife.

30 green walnuts
2 sticks cinnamon
5 whole cloves
One 1-inch piece vanilla bean

Zest of 1 lemon, removed with a vegetable peeler
2½ cups sugar
1 liter vodka

1   Rinse and dry the walnuts. Quarter them with a chef's knife or cleaver. Keep the fingers of your other hand on top of the knife and away from the blade.

2   Put the walnuts in a large glass container along with the cinnamon, cloves, vanilla bean, lemon zest, and sugar. Add the vodka to cover the walnuts. Cover and let stand 6 to 8 weeks, agitating the container daily.

3   When ready to bottle, remove and discard the walnuts. Filter the nocino through cheesecloth, pour into clean bottles, and cork tightly. Nocino will keep for several years stored in a cool, dry place.

Le livre
des
Confitures

PINEAPPLE GINGER MARMALADE

5 CUPS

I make this whenever my marmalade supply is running low, since good pineapples are almost always in season. The candied ginger gives breakfast a lift and the little bit of rum effectively complements my morning coffee.

1 pineapple
1 navel orange
10 cups water
5 cups sugar

6 tablespoons (3 ounces) chopped candied ginger (page 165)
1 tablespoon dark rum

1   Peel and remove the eyes from the pineapple. Quarter the pineapple and remove the core. Dice the pineapple flesh into ½-inch pieces.

2   Quarter the orange, then slice the unpeeled quarters as thin as possible.

3   With a chef's knife or a food processor, roughly chop the pineapple and orange into ¼-inch pieces.

4   Put the chopped fruits in a heavy nonreactive 8-quart pot. Add the water, bring to a simmer, and cook for 30 minutes. Remove from the heat, cover, and set aside for a few hours or overnight.

5   To finish the marmalade, add the sugar, bring to a boil, and cook over medium to high heat until it reaches the jelling point, about 220 degrees. To test the marmalade, turn off the heat and put a small amount on a plate that has been chilled in the freezer. Return the plate to the freezer, and check after a few minutes by nudging it with your finger. If it wrinkles, it has jelled. If you are using a candy thermometer, the jam will set at around 220 degrees, but it should still be tested on a chilled plate.

6   Stir in the chopped candied ginger and rum. Ladle the marmalade into clean jars. If you can't refrigerate the marmalade, use sterilized jars, properly sealed. Otherwise, pack it into clean jars, let it cool, and store in the refrigerator, tightly covered, for up to 1 year.

SEVILLE ORANGE MARMALADE

2 QUARTS

I love this marmalade, but I might not have started making it every year if it hadn't been for the two charming women in Miami Beach to whom I once gave a jar as a gift. They liked it so much that they insisted I make it again the next year, and now making this marmalade has become an annual tradition for me. I always send them a jar from my first, which is sometimes my only, batch.

The many seeds in sour oranges contain a great deal of pectin, which helps the marmalade jell properly. A sharp serrated knife works best for slicing the oranges very thin. If you're impatient, process the oranges briefly in a food processor. The marmalade will taste the same, but you won't get the lovely effect of the brilliant orange slices suspended in jelled syrup.

6 Seville oranges, or other sour oranges, preferably organic
1 navel orange
10 cups water

8 cups sugar
Optional: 2 tablespoons Cognac or Scotch

1   Rinse the oranges and wipe them dry. Slice the stem ends off all the oranges, cut them in half crosswise through the equator, and remove the seeds with the tip of a paring knife. Tie the seeds together in a piece of cheesecloth. Cut each orange half in half and slice as thin as possible.

2   Put the orange slices in a heavy nonreactive 8-quart pot and add the water and the cheesecloth bag of seeds. Cover and let stand overnight.

3   The next day, stir the sugar into the mixture and set the stockpot over high heat. Bring the oranges to a boil, then reduce the heat to maintain a gentle boil. Stir occasionally while they cook to make sure they are not burning on the bottom. If white scum occasionally rises to the top, skim it off with a large spoon and discard it.

4   Continue cooking until the marmalade reaches the jelling point, 220 degrees. It will probably take at least 1 hour. At this point, turn off the heat, and put a small amount on a plate that has been chilled in the freezer. Return the plate to the freezer, and after a few minutes, check it by nudging it with your finger. If it wrinkles, it has jelled. Add the optional Cognac or Scotch to the marmalade after it has finished cooking.

5   Remove the cheesecloth bag of seeds and ladle the mixture into clean jars. If you can't refrigerate the marmalade, use sterilized jars, properly sealed. However, I simply pack it into clean jars, let it cool, and store it in the refrigerator, tightly covered, for up to 1 year.

PLUM STRAWBERRY JAM

1 QUART

One 1-pint basket strawberries
1 pound red plums (about 10),
such as Santa Rosa

2¼ cups sugar

One summer afternoon at a party, while everyone else was enjoying the sunshine and their libations, I was climbing my hosts' Santa Rosa plum tree (in my Japanese designer pants!) and eating as many of them as I could. The plums were so good we planned another party the next day in my kitchen to make jam, but I was a little startled when my friends showed up with four cases of plums: I hadn't counted on quite such a massive party.

Tossing the fruit with sugar and letting it stand for a few hours intensifies the color of the strawberries, and the jam will be a vivid brilliant red. It's always better to make jam in small batches; that way the jam retains more flavor and color and it is easier to monitor and control the rate of jelling. Although strawberries are low in pectin, plums have lots of it, so this recipe will produce a jam that is wonderfully chunky with a great jell.

1   Rinse and hull the strawberries. Cut the berries in half lengthwise, and slice the halves into ¼-inch-thick slices.

2   Wash the plums. Cut them in half, remove the pits, and slice the plums into ¼-inch-thick slices.

3   Toss the strawberries and plums with the sugar in a heavy nonreactive pan that holds at least 6 quarts. Let stand for a minimum of 1 hour, tossing occasionally to encourage the fruits to release their juices.

4   Bring the fruits and sugar to the boil. As they cook, skim off any thick whitish foam that rises to the surface, and stir occasionally to prevent the fruit from burning on the bottom of the pan. Put a small plate in the freezer for testing the jam later.

5   When the jam thickens somewhat, remove it from the heat and put a spoonful on the cold plate. Return the plate to the freezer. After a minute, check it by nudging it with your finger. If it wrinkles, it has jelled. If you are using a candy thermometer, the jam will set at around 220 degrees, but should still be tested on a chilled plate to make sure it has set.

6   Ladle the jam into clean jars. If you can't refrigerate it, use sterilized jars, properly sealed. Otherwise, pour it into clean jars, let it cool, and store it in the refrigerator, tightly covered, for up to 1 year.

Note: If you are inexperienced at making jam, test it frequently, even before you think it may be done. It doesn't harm the jam to turn it off and on, but once it has cooked too far, the sugar will caramelize and the jam will have an unpleasant flavor and be beyond redemption.

FIG JAM

1 QUART

Fig jam has delightful little crackly seeds in it, like poppy seeds, because fig seeds don't soften when they cook.

3 pounds fresh, ripe figs
½ **cup water**

3 cups sugar
¼ **cup lemon juice**

1   Rinse the figs and remove the hard stems. Slice the figs into quarters.

2   Simmer the figs with the water in a heavy saucepan, covered, until they are completely cooked, about 15 minutes. They should be quite soft and tender.

3   Purée the figs in a food processor or pass them through a food mill.

4   Transfer the fig purée back into the saucepan. Stir in the sugar and lemon juice.

5   Cook the sweetened purée until thickened, stirring constantly to prevent scorching on the bottom. Because figs have a lot of natural sugar, fig jam tends to cook very quickly. The jam will appear slightly jelled when ready.

6   Ladle the jam into clean jars. If you can't refrigerate the jam, use sterilized jars, properly sealed. Otherwise, simply pack it into clean jars, let it cool, and store it in the refrigerator, tightly covered.

CANDIED CHERRIES

ABOUT 1 QUART

A good way to preserve a
bumper crop from the all-too-
short cherry season. Spoon a
few candied cherries over ice
cream, or drain off the liquid,
chop them up, and fold them
into ice cream. They are
especially good served with
chocolate gelato (page 125).

Try to use sour cherries if you
can get them: they are
excellent when candied. If
sour cherries are unavailable,
sweet cherries are fine. I
usually cook them with lemon
to heighten their flavor and
cut their sweetness a bit.
Candied cherries keep for up
to a year in the refrigerator.

1 pound fresh cherries   ½ **lemon**
2 cups sugar   **1 cup apple juice**
½ **cup water**

1   Rinse the cherries and remove the pits. In a nonreactive
saucepan, bring the sugar and water to a boil. Add the cherries
and the lemon half.

2   Reduce the heat to a simmer and cook until the syrup turns
red and is slightly thick, about 20 minutes. Cover and let stand
2 to 3 hours or overnight.

3   Strain the cherries, reserving the syrup, and set them aside.
Discard the lemon half and add the apple juice to the syrup. Bring
the syrup to a boil and cook for 5 minutes. Return the cherries to
the syrup, reduce the heat, and cook at a slow boil until the syrup
is thick and the temperature is about 220 degrees.

4   Remove from the heat and cool. Transfer the candied cherries
and their syrup into a jar, cool to room temperature, cover, and
store in the refrigerator.

Baking requires more precision than, say, making soup. Baking requires you to measure things. No one can expect to improve on most of the classic formulas by taking liberties with these measurements, because many basic pastry recipes are based on chemical reactions for which the optimal ratios of ingredients are pretty much known.

But once you've mastered a few of the basic elements of desserts—once you can make a buttery pie crust confidently, or a suave crème anglaise or sabayon, for example—there's no need to rein in your imagination: Try a new kind of fruit pie; offer two fruit sauces instead of one; serve crème anglaise with something as simple as a bowl of berries or sliced peaches. The recipes in this chapter are the basics. Learning them will enable you to make any number of impromptu combinations.

BASICS

TART DOUGH

ABOUT 10 OUNCES DOUGH, ENOUGH FOR ONE 9-INCH TART

This is the recipe I use for all the tarts I bake in tart pans. This tart dough is sturdy enough, but still crumbly; and it's easy to roll out. I worked out the recipe with the help of expert baker Flo Braker, who patiently answered my frantic phone calls during an exhaustive bout of tart dough experimentation. Flo's criteria for a perfect dough are straightforward: The dough has to be easy to make and it should not shrink during baking. This one fills the bill.

6 tablespoons (¾ stick) butter, at room temperature

¼ cup sugar

1 egg yolk

1 cup flour

⅛ teaspoon salt

1   In the bowl of an electric mixer, beat the butter and sugar together at low speed for about 1 minute, until they are just creamed together but not aerated.

2   Add the egg and continue mixing another 30 seconds. The mixture will look curdled, but it will come together when the flour is added.

3   Mix together the flour and the salt, add to the mixing bowl, and mix until the dough comes together in a smooth, homogeneous mass. Gather the dough and form it into a disk about 1 inch thick. Wrap in plastic wrap and refrigerate for at least 30 minutes.

4   To roll out the dough, remove it from the refrigerator. The dough should be cold but malleable. If it's very firm, whack the sides of the dough on the counter to soften it and prevent it from cracking. If the dough has been refrigerated longer, let it soften for a couple of minutes first.

5   Roll the dough on a lightly floured surface. Lift the dough frequently to make sure it isn't sticking, and add a dusting of flour to the work surface if it is. Be careful to use no more flour than is necessary, brushing off any excess. Roll out the dough into a 12- to 14-inch circle.

6   Fold the circle in half and lift it into a 9-inch tart pan with a removable bottom, placing the folded edge at the center of the pan. Unfold the dough and with your fingers coax the dough tightly into the corner, where the bottom meets the sides of the pan, and up against the sides, being careful not to stretch the dough. Press the dough firmly against the sides of the pan. Roll the rolling pin over the edge of the tart pan to shear off excess dough. Refrigerate or freeze the tart shell for at least 20 minutes.

7   To bake, position the oven rack in the lower third of the oven and preheat the oven to 375 degrees.

8   Prick the dough five or six times with the tines of a fork. Line the tart shell with a piece of aluminum foil, fill halfway with pie weights (see page 6), and bake the shell for about 20 minutes, or until golden brown throughout. When done, remove from the oven, remove the weights and the foil, and allow to cool completely on a rack before filling.

Note: Tart dough can be well wrapped and frozen for a month or so, either in its unrolled state or already rolled out and lining a tart pan. Once it's baked, though, I'm adamant about serving it the same day, so although the dough can be made well in advance, don't bake it until you need it.

PIE DOUGH

1½ POUNDS PIE DOUGH, ENOUGH FOR ONE 9-INCH OR 10-INCH
DOUBLE-CRUST PIE OR TWO 9-INCH OR 10-INCH SINGLE-CRUST PIES

For pies, I like the taste of butter, and therefore I like all-butter pie crust. In my opinion, if you're going to eat fat, it had better be butter and not vegetable shortening. Handled properly, butter crust is always flaky.

2½ cups flour
½ teaspoon salt
1 tablespoon sugar

½ pound (2 sticks) butter, cut into cubes about 1 inch square and refrigerated
6 to 8 tablespoons ice water

1   Mix together the flour, salt, and sugar. Use an electric mixer equipped with a paddle attachment, a food processor, or a hand-held wire pastry blender.

2   Add the chilled butter to the dry ingredients and continue mixing just long enough for the cubes of butter to become incorporated into the flour and broken up into roughly ¼-inch-size pieces. Add 6 tablespoons of the ice water all at once and continue mixing until the dough just begins to hold itself together. If necessary, use the remaining 2 tablespoons water.

3   Form the dough into two balls. Wrap each one in plastic, and flatten them into disks about 1 inch thick. Refrigerate for at least 1 hour before rolling out.

4   To roll out and prebake a 9- or 10-inch single-crust pie shell, roll out one of the disks of dough into a circle 14 inches in diameter. Fold in half and place in a 9- or 10-inch pie dish (I prefer an ovenproof glass pie plate to a metal pie pan). Unfold the dough, centering it, and gently press it snugly into the dish with your fingers. Cut away dough that is overhanging the edge of the pie plate with a sharp paring knife. Put in the freezer for about 30 minutes.

5   Position the oven rack in the lower part of the oven and preheat the oven to 375 degrees.

6   Remove the pie shell from the freezer, line with a piece of aluminum foil, fill halfway with pie weights (see page 6), and bake for about 20 minutes, until the bottom of the crust begins to brown. Remove the weights and the foil and continue baking for another 10 minutes, until the shell is completely browned.

7   To roll out, fill, and bake a double-crust pie, first have your filling ready. Position the oven rack in the center of the oven, and preheat the oven to 375 degrees.

8   On a lightly floured surface, roll out one of the disks of dough into a circle 14 inches in diameter. Fold it in half and drape it into a 9- or 10-inch pie dish. Unfold the dough, centering it, and gently press it snugly into the dish with your fingers. Cut away dough that is overhanging the edge of the pie plate with a sharp paring knife. Add the prepared filling, smoothing it evenly in the shell.

9   Roll out the other disk of dough into another 14-inch circle. Dip a pastry brush or your fingers in water and moisten the exposed edges of the dough in the pie tin. Center the other piece of dough over the filled pie tin. Working all the way around the pie, lift the lower crust and tuck the edges of the upper crust between the edge of the lower crust and the rim of the pie tin. Work your way around the pie again, crimping the edges decoratively by repeatedly pressing downward with one thumb, while from the side, the forefinger and thumb of the other hand pinch the dough around the thumb pressing down.

10 Bake the pie in the preheated oven for 50 to 60 minutes, until the top is browned and the filling juices are thick and bubbling. Cool before serving.

Note: If the dough is frozen or refrigerated for more than an hour before you roll it out, let it sit at room temperature for about 5 minutes, until it becomes slightly malleable again.

GALETTE DOUGH

ABOUT 9 OUNCES DOUGH, ENOUGH FOR ONE GALETTE OR TART, 10 TO 12 INCHES IN DIAMETER

Whenever I teach or give demonstrations, most of my audience admits to a terror of making dough. I use this recipe to help them overcome it. Galette dough is the workhorse in my repertoire. It is sturdy, but still flaky and easy to roll out without breaking or shrinking. It's used for making the free-form tarts known as galettes. Fruit tarts made with it have a rustic appeal because the dough is usually rolled out flat, filled with sliced fruits, and the edges are folded partway back over the fruit to contain it during baking.

1 cup flour
2 teaspoons sugar
¼ teaspoon salt

6 tablespoons (¾ stick) butter, chilled and cut into 1-inch cubes
3 to 4 tablespoons ice water

1   Mix together the flour, sugar, and salt. Use an electric mixer, a pastry blender, or your hands.

2   Add the butter and continue mixing until the butter is partially broken up but still very chunky.

3   Add 3 tablespoons of the ice water and mix until the dough just comes together. If it seems too dry you may need to add the additional tablespoon of ice water.

4   Gather the dough with your hands, shape it into a disk, wrap it in plastic, and refrigerate for at least 30 minutes, or until you're ready to roll it out. Or you can freeze it at this point.

PÂTE À CHOUX

20 TO 25 PUFFS

Use pâte à choux to make cream puffs piped full of Meyer lemon curd (page 40) or split in half, filled with scoops of your favorite ice cream, and topped with chocolate sauce (page 196) or rich caramel sauce (page 194).

Pâte à choux can also easily be made into great appetizer cheese puffs: Before you pipe out the dough, stir in 1 cup of grated Gruyère or some sharper cheese, and perhaps some chopped herbs, or good-quality salt-packed anchovies, rinsed, filleted, and chopped very fine.

Note: Puffs can be stored at room temperature for several hours, or frozen, defrosted, and warmed for a few minutes in a 350-degree oven.

1 cup water
¼ teaspoon salt
2 teaspoons sugar
6 tablespoons (¾ stick) butter, cut into ½-inch cubes

1 cup flour
4 eggs

1   Position the oven rack in the center of the oven. Preheat the oven to 425 degrees.

2   Bring the water, salt, sugar, and butter to the boil in a large heavy saucepan over medium heat, stirring frequently.

3   When the mixture begins to boil, add the flour all at once and stir continuously with a wooden spoon until the paste forms a ball and comes away from the sides of the pan.

4   Remove from the heat. Wait a minute, then begin beating the mixture, either by hand or, preferably, in a standing electric mixer with a paddle attachment. Beat in the eggs, one at a time, making sure each one is fully incorporated before adding the next. The dough should be stiff and shiny. I break the eggs into a bowl first to make sure no eggshell gets into the pâte à choux.

5   Pipe the pâte à choux from a pastry bag onto parchment-lined baking sheets (or drop by spoonfuls) in 1½-inch-high mounds, at 3-inch intervals. When piping out this dough, the action of lifting the pastry bag often leaves a little point on each unbaked puff. To prevent them from burning, flatten any points with a dampened finger. Put the baking sheets into the oven and lower the heat to 375 degrees.

6   Bake the puffs for 25 to 30 minutes, until they are golden brown, both on top and up the sides. (If they are not fully cooked, they will collapse as they cool.) Remove them from the oven and turn the oven off.

7   Poke each puff in the side with a knife to release steam, which will otherwise make them soggy. Return the puffs to the turned-off oven for 5 minutes. Cool.

SPONGE CAKE

This very good sponge cake recipe was given to me by the ever-gracious Shirley Sarvis, a food writer and a first-rate baker. When I asked her the reason for adding water to sponge cake batter, she replied, "For moisture, of course!"

5 eggs, separated, at room temperature

½ cup cold water

1½ cups sugar

1 teaspoon vanilla extract

1½ cups cake flour

½ teaspoon baking powder

¼ teaspoon salt

1   Position the oven rack in the center of the oven and preheat the oven to 350 degrees. Lightly butter only the bottom of a 12 by 18-inch sheet pan or a 9 by 3-inch round cake pan. Either cover it with a sheet of parchment paper or dust it with flour and tap out any excess.

2   In an electric mixer running at medium speed, whip together the egg yolks and the water for 1 minute. Lower the mixer speed and add the sugar and vanilla extract, then increase the mixer speed to high and continue beating for 5 minutes, until a ribbon forms when you lift the whip.

3   While the egg yolks and sugar are beating, sift together the flour, baking powder, and salt.

4   Once the egg yolks form a ribbon, beat the egg whites in another bowl, until they form soft drooping peaks when you lift the beater.

5   Incorporate the flour mixture into the egg yolk mixture by sifting the dry ingredients over the yolks with one hand and fold-ing with a whisk with the other. Set the bowl on a damp towel to steady it while you sift and fold. When the flour is completely incorporated, use a rubber spatula to fold in the beaten egg whites.

6   Pour the batter into the prepared sheet pan or cake pan and spread it quickly in an even layer with an offset metal spatula or a rubber spatula.

7   Bake for 15 to 18 minutes in a sheet pan, or about 45 min-utes in a cake pan, until the top is brown and the cake springs back when you touch it. Store at room temperature.

Note: Sponge cake is easier to slice if made a day in advance.

PASTRY CREAM

ABOUT 1 CUP

About the only thing I ever use pastry cream for is as a base for soufflés or as a filling for napoleons, lightened with whipped cream. But you may want to use pastry cream as a creamy base for fresh fruit tarts or as a filling for cream puffs or layer cakes, flavored with liqueurs or citrus zest or chocolate.

1 cup milk
3 tablespoons flour
4 tablespoons sugar

3 egg yolks
¼ teaspoon vanilla extract

1   Warm the milk in a saucepan. Meanwhile whisk together the flour and sugar in a bowl.

2   When the milk is hot and begins to steam, whisk in the flour and sugar. Cook over moderate heat, whisking, until the mixture is thickened, about 2 minutes. Be sure to use a whisk: The mixture tends to get lumpy and a whisk is the best tool for smoothing out lumps.

3   Lightly beat the egg yolks and then whisk in some of the hot milk mixture to warm the yolks. Add the warmed yolks to the thickened milk and cook, stirring constantly, until the pastry cream just begins to boil. Remove from the heat and strain into a container. Stir in the vanilla extract. Cover snugly with plastic wrap and refrigerate for up to 3 days.

FRANGIPANE

ABOUT 1 CUP

Spreading a layer of frangipane to form a base for a fruit tart not only adds the wonderful flavor of almond, it also keeps the tart dough from getting soggy from the fruit juices.

3 ounces almond paste
3 tablespoons butter, at room temperature

1½ teaspoons sugar
1½ tablespoons flour
1 egg

In a mixing bowl, beat together the almond paste, butter, sugar, and flour. Beat in the egg until completely mixed. Use immediately or store in the refrigerator for up to 2 weeks. Bring to room temperature before using.

CRÈME ANGLAISE

2½ CUPS

Very early menus at Chez Panisse sometimes offered this classic dessert sauce all by itself—by the glass, as a drink!

Crème anglaise can be flavored by steeping toasted, chopped nuts and spices like cinnamon or cloves in the warm milk—or more easily by adding espresso or Cognac, rum, or any other tasty liquor to the sauce after it has cooled.

½ **vanilla bean, split**
2 **cups milk**
6 **tablespoons sugar**

Pinch of salt
6 **egg yolks**

1   Scrape the vanilla bean seeds into the milk in a heavy saucepan. Add the vanilla bean pod, sugar, and salt and heat until the milk is warm but not simmering. Meanwhile, prepare an ice bath—a bowl partially filled with ice, with another bowl nested inside it.

2   Lightly whisk together the egg yolks in a separate bowl, then gradually add some of the warmed milk, whisking constantly. Pour the mixture back into the saucepan.

3   Cook over low to moderate heat, stirring constantly with a heatproof spatula, always scraping the bottom, until the custard thickens enough to coat the spatula.

4   Immediately strain the cooked custard through a fine sieve into the bowl set in the ice. Stir the crème anglaise with a clean spatula to cool it down. Cover and refrigerate until ready to serve. Crème anglaise will keep in the refrigerator for up to 3 days.

Note: If you accidentally overcook crème anglaise and it looks curdled after you've strained it, you can still rescue it. Pour it into a blender while it's still warm, filling the container no more than halfway, and run at low speed until it looks smooth.

CHAMPAGNE SABAYON

ABOUT 3½ CUPS

Sabayon *and* zabaglione *are the French and Italian names, respectively, for the same thing: sweetened egg yolks flavored with wine, thickened and beaten to an ethereal lightness over low heat, and served either cold—as in this recipe, with whipped cream folded in—or hot, without the cream. Don't limit yourself to sabayon flavored with Champagne. In Italy the traditional flavoring is Marsala, but any good white wine or fortified wine, dry or sweet, will make good sabayon. Served over fresh berries, it is sublime.*

This recipe makes sabayon by a somewhat untraditional method: Instead of mixing together the egg yolks, sugar, and wine at the outset and beating entirely by hand over a hot stove, the egg yolks are first thickened with an electric mixer, the wine and sugar are heated separately and beaten into the eggs by machine, and only then is the mixture finished over the stove, by hand.

7 egg yolks
¹/₃ cup sugar

²/₃ cup Champagne
½ cup heavy cream

1   Begin beating the egg yolks in an electric mixer on high speed. Have an ice bath ready—a bowl of ice with another bowl nested inside it.

2   In a large saucepan, heat the sugar and the Champagne until almost at the boil.

3   When the egg yolks have thickened, continue beating while slowly pouring in the hot wine and sugar.

4   Transfer the egg yolk mixture from the mixer back into the saucepan. Whisk vigorously over low to moderate heat until the sabayon has thickened enough that it holds its shape when you lift the whisk. The sabayon thickens quickly—be sure not to overcook.

5   Immediately pour the sabayon into the bowl in the ice bath to cool it down, stirring occasionally.

6   Whip the cream until it forms very soft peaks and fold it into the egg mixture. Refrigerated, sabayon will keep up to 24 hours.

WHIPPED CREAM

2 CUPS

Use the freshest cream available. If possible, avoid using ultrapasteurized cream: It has practically no cream flavor.

1 cup heavy cream
1 tablespoon sugar

A few drops of vanilla extract
Optional: ¼ vanilla bean

1   With an electric mixer or by hand with a whisk, whip the cream until it just begins to hold a shape.

2   Whip in the sugar and add the vanilla extract. If desired, split the vanilla bean and scrape its seeds into the cream.

3   Continue to whip the cream until it is soft and creamy, mounding gently. Do not whip it until it is stiff, or it will be grainy.

Note: If you make whipped cream in advance, it may be necessary to rewhip it very slightly just before serving, since the cream separates as it sits.

If you overwhip the cream by accident, you can save it by gently folding in small amounts of unwhipped heavy cream until it smooths out.

COGNAC CARAMEL SAUCE

ABOUT 1½ CUPS

This thin but very flavorful sauce is useful for drizzling over desserts. If you caramelize the sugar to the point just before it begins to burn, the sauce will have a deep caramel flavor. If you wish, you can use bourbon, rum, or another favorite liquor instead of Cognac.

1 cup sugar
⅓ cup water, plus ½ cup for stopping caramelization

Pinch of cream of tartar, or a few drops lemon juice
¾ cup Cognac

1   See the caramelization guidelines on page 200. Spread the sugar in the bottom of a sauté pan or a saucepan with a heavy bottom. Pour the ⅓ cup of water over the sugar to moisten it.

2   Cook the sugar and water over low heat until the sugar dissolves, then increase the heat and bring the mixture to a boil. Add the cream of tartar or lemon juice.

3   Continue to cook the sugar without stirring, until the sugar begins to turn a light amber color, which is the beginning of caramelization.

4   Keep a constant eye on the caramel as it will cook very fast at this point. When the caramel turns a dark amber color and begins to smoke, turn off the heat and immediately add the additional ½ cup of water.

5   Stir the caramel to dissolve any lumps of caramelized sugar and allow it to cool for 5 minutes. Once it has cooled down a bit, stir in the Cognac. This sauce can be stored indefinitely at room temperature until ready to use, and rewarmed over very low heat.

RICH CARAMEL SAUCE

ABOUT 1½ CUPS

It's important to stop the caramel at just the right moment before it burns. Have the heavy cream ready and if the phone rings, don't answer it.

8 tablespoons (1 stick) salted butter

1 cup sugar

1 cup heavy cream

¼ teaspoon vanilla extract

1   See the caramelization guidelines on page 200. Melt the butter in a large saucepan (see Note). Stir in the sugar and cook over medium heat, stirring occasionally with a heatproof utensil, until the mixture begins to caramelize and turn an amber color. When the caramel has turned somewhat reddish and has begun to smoke, watch carefully, and just when it looks and smells as if it is about to burn, remove from the heat and quickly pour in the heavy cream.

2   Stir the caramel until the sauce is smooth and creamy. Add the vanilla. Cover and store the caramel sauce in the refrigerator, for up to 1 week. Rewarm before serving.

Note: The caramel will bubble up when the heavy cream is added, so it is important that you use a large enough saucepan for this recipe.

ORANGE CARAMEL SAUCE

ABOUT 1 CUP

I make this with blood orange juice, when it is available, because it gives the sauce such a vivid color. The few drops of orange juice in the sugar help prevent the caramel from crystallizing.

1 cup plus 2 tablespoons sugar
6 tablespoons water

½ cup orange juice, plus ¼ cup to stop caramelization

1   See the caramelization guidelines on page 200. Spread the sugar evenly in a heavy-duty saucepan or sauté pan. Add the water and a few of drops of the orange juice and cook over low heat until the sugar is dissolved.

2   Increase the heat and cook until the sugar turns a dark amber color and just begins to smoke. Remove from heat and pour in ¼ cup of the orange juice to stop the caramelization. Swirl the pan to dissolve the caramel with the orange juice. Let cool for 1 minute, then whisk in the remaining ½ cup orange juice. Strain, then cool completely, cover, and refrigerate until use. It will keep for at least a month.

CHOCOLATE SAUCE

ABOUT 3½ CUPS

I like my chocolate sauce slick, dark, and bitter, with a beautiful sheen. Once cooled, this sauce can be swirled into a homemade ice cream that you've just frozen.

2 cups water
½ cup light corn syrup
1½ cups cocoa (preferably Dutch-processed)

1 cup sugar
4 ounces bittersweet chocolate

1   Heat together the water and corn syrup in a saucepan. Whisk together the cocoa and sugar in a bowl and add them to the hot water. Bring to a boil, whisking frequently to break up any lumps of cocoa and to prevent the bottom from burning. Remove from the heat.

2   Coarsely chop the chocolate and stir it into the warm cocoa mixture. Whisk until the chocolate is melted. Cool and refrigerate. This sauce keeps for up to 1 month under refrigeration. It is best made a few hours or a day ahead of when you plan to use it, to allow time for the cocoa to thicken the sauce properly, and rewarmed in a double boiler before serving.

SOFT CANDIED CITRUS PEEL

Thin candied strips of citrus peel enliven the flavor of desserts and look beautiful, too, garnishing fruit compotes, sherbets, custards, and especially the shimmering Champagne gelée (page 130).

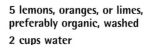

5 lemons, oranges, or limes, preferably organic, washed

2 cups water

1 cup sugar

1 tablespoon light corn syrup

1   Remove the thin layer of colored zest from the lemons, oranges, or limes with a vegetable peeler, being careful to leave behind the bitter white skin beneath.

2   With a sharp knife, cut the pieces of peel lengthwise into very thin thread-like strips.

3   Put the peel in a saucepan, add enough water to cover generously, bring to a boil, and cook until the peel is soft and translucent, 5 to 6 minutes.

4   Drain the peel and discard the water. In the same saucepan, bring 2 cups of water, the sugar, and corn syrup to the boil. Add the drained peel, reduce the heat to a simmer, and cook until the peel is translucent and candied, about 20 minutes. The syrup will have thickened and reduced significantly and the temperature will register 210 degrees on a candy thermometer. Cool, transfer the peel to a container, cover, and refrigerate until ready to use. The peel will keep for 2 months at least.

Note: If the syrup has thickened so much after refrigeration that you can't remove the peel, or if the syrup has crystallized, reheat the peel in the syrup with a few tablespoons of water.

Variation: *At Lindsey Shere's suggestion, I once added a few drops of grenadine to the syrup while the peel was being candied, coloring it a vivid red. A few drops of cassis or another compatible fruit syrup would do the same.*

BLACKBERRY SAUCE

1 CUP

A very shiny, deep-colored sauce that is especially good with vanilla ice cream.

One 1-pint basket blackberries (2 cups)

3 tablespoons sugar
¼ teaspoon lemon juice

Purée the berries through a food mill or in a food processor and press them through a fine-mesh sieve to remove their seeds. Whisk in the sugar and lemon juice, whisking until the sugar dissolves. Taste for sweetness and adjust, if necessary.

RASPBERRY SAUCE

1 CUP

This is a good way to use raspberries that no longer look pristine—after you carefully pick over them, of course. These days, chefs who make elaborate plated desserts are likely to put raspberry sauce on absolutely everything. I still like using it for Pavlova, for instance (page 100), or to sauce cream puffs, vanilla ice cream, and chocolate soufflés, or swirled into a vanilla soufflé right before you bake it. And I like it on the table in a little pitcher so you can pour on more if you want.

One 1-pint basket raspberries (2 cups)
1½ tablespoons sugar
¼ cup water

½ teaspoon lemon juice
Optional: 1 teaspoon kirsch or framboise

1   Pass the raspberries through a food mill fitted with a fine disk, or purée the raspberries in a food processor and press through a sieve to remove the seeds.

2   Heat the sugar and the water together until the sugar is dissolved. Stir it into the raspberry purée and add the lemon juice and the kirsch or framboise, if desired.

3   Taste and, if necessary, adjust with additional sugar, lemon juice, or kirsch or framboise.

STRAWBERRY SAUCE

1 CUP

I don't necessarily strain all
*the seeds out, since
sometimes I like their texture
and appearance in the sauce.*

One 1-pint basket strawberries   **1 teaspoon lemon juice or kirsch**
2 tablespoons sugar

Purée the berries in a food processor with the sugar and the
lemon juice or kirsch. Press the sauce through a fine-mesh sieve
to remove the seeds. Taste for sweetness and adjust, if necessary.

MANGO SAUCE

1¼ CUPS

*The mango varieties most
commonly available where I
live are the Hayden and
Tommy Atkins mangoes
imported from Mexico. These
are sweeter than many other
varieties, so I always start
with the smaller amount of
sugar and add more if
necessary.*

1 medium mango   **1½ teaspoons rum**
1 tablespoon water   **2 teaspoons lime juice**
2 to 4 tablespoons sugar

Peel the mango and cut the flesh away from the pit. Cut the pulp
into small pieces and purée with the water, sugar, rum, and lime
juice in a food processor or a blender. Taste for sweetness and flavor and adjust, if necessary.

APPENDIX

CARAMELIZATION GUIDELINES

Sugar is said to be caramelized when it is melted and cooked until it colors. There are two ways to do this: the "wet" method, in which the sugar is cooked with water added, and the "dry" method, in which the sugar is cooked without water. In both methods, the sugar is cooked until it melts, darkens, and turns a rich deep brown color. Caramelized sugar is used to flavor sauces, custards, soufflés, ice creams, and candies. I use it often because it adds a very full flavor without necessarily adding discernible extra sweetness.

Only granulated sugar can be successfully caramelized; brown sugar and powdered sugar contain impurities that inhibit caramelization. I recommend using cane sugar (always clearly labeled on the package). Compared to beet sugar, cane sugar reportedly contains fewer of the impurities that may impede smooth caramelization.

When caramelizing sugar, give it your undivided attention. Not only can the sugar go quickly from clear liquid to burnt syrup, but it is *very* hot, over 350 degrees, and if so much as a drop lands on your skin you will receive a painful burn. Therefore, observe these safety precautions whenever you make caramel:

1:    Have everything ready before you begin. Be sure all utensils are very clean, since a small food particle can cause your caramel to crystallize. A wooden spoon or spatula is best for stirring; it will neither melt nor become too hot to handle. Heat-resistant rubber spatulas can supposedly withstand heats of up to 475 degrees. Nevertheless, be wary: Stirring hot caramel, I once melted a spoon whose label boasted that it had been "specially designed for caramelization." The liquid you plan to add to stop the caramelizing should be ready and at hand.

2:    Use an unlined metal pot or pan: Heat can permanently damage linings. Tin-lined copper pots are particularly vulnerable. I prefer heavy-duty stainless steel All-Clad brand cookware, in part because it's easier to judge the color of the sugar inside a bright stainless steel pan than it is in a cast iron one. Furthermore, the handles don't get hot and the bottoms don't ever warp.

3:    Keep a sizable container of ice water handy. If you accidentally spill hot caramel on your hand, immediately plunge it into the ice water to stop the burn. One caramel burn is usually all it takes to make you more careful the next time you work with caramel.

4:    Adding liquid to hot caramelized sugar can cause splattering and bubbling up in a pot. Always choose a pot big enough to contain plenty of expansion. When adding liquid, pour it through a strainer inverted over the pot. This will disperse the liquid and partially shield you from splattering caramel and steam. You can protect your hands by wearing long oven mitts. It's also good to stand back and avert your face as you pour.

The darker the caramel, the better the flavor—so long as it's not burnt. A caramel that hasn't been cooked enough will have a weak flavor and just taste sweet; one that is burned must be discarded. My rule of thumb is to cook the caramel to the point where it has turned a dark amber color and is just beginning to smoke. At this point I hover, watching carefully. You may want to remove the sugar from the heat now, since it will continue to cook, but more slowly, giving you more control. In a few seconds, the caramel will go from brown to a reddish brown about the same color as an old penny. I use my sense of smell, checking constantly until I recognize the point at which it is almost beginning to burn. Then I immediately stop the caramelization with whatever liquid I am using.

It may take a little practice to master caramelizing sugar, but it's usually easy once you've done it a couple of times. Use low heat if you're a beginner and remember, even very experienced pastry chefs sometimes overcook and burn caramel and have to start over again.

WET CARAMEL

When making caramel, your main nemesis will be sugar's natural tendency to crystallize. Your first object is to melt the sugar crystals, and when they are liquefied, you want to prevent crystals from re-forming. Since crystal molecules have jagged edges, they naturally want to regroup and lock together, and that is the last thing you want to have happen. Stirring a wet caramel encourages the molecules to bump up against each other and reattach themselves. When they start piling up, the chain reaction won't stop until the sugar resolidifies. Any foreign particle in the melted sugar can also provide a starting point for recrystallization.

One common technique for preventing crystallization is to cook the sugar in a covered pot until the sugar is completely melted: The trapped condensation washes away crystals clinging to the side of the pot. Another is to use a clean brush dipped in water to wash down the sides, dissolving any crystals. I don't recommend this technique, because I always end up losing a few bristles in the caramel.

The best preventive is adding an interfering agent: a tiny amount of an acid like cream of tartar or lemon juice, which will "invert" the sugar, rearranging its molecular structure so that it loses its natural tendency to crystallize.

Begin by adding sugar to the pot in an even layer. Pour water over the sugar until it is completely saturated and there are no dry spots. Avoid splashing any sugar granules on the sides of the pot, which could lead to troublesome crystallization later. Heat until the sugar dissolves. Add a pinch of cream of tartar or a few drops of lemon juice. Continue cooking, watching carefully as the sugar begins to brown. When it has darkened to the point of being almost burnt, stop the cooking by pouring in the liquid called for in the recipe. After the liquid is added, the caramel can be stirred or whisked until smooth.

If for some reason the caramel begins to crystallize before you add the liquid, you can continue to cook it; however, much of the sugar will not color and you won't get the full flavor that you are looking for.

DRY CARAMEL

This is actually easier than the wet method in some ways, but it can be difficult to control the rate of caramelization since it happens so quickly. First sprinkle an even layer of sugar in a pot, preferably a wide-bottomed one. As you slowly heat the sugar, the edges and bottom will melt and cook first. To promote even melting, stir the sugar gently with a heatproof utensil, or tilt and swirl the pan. The sugar will caramelize rapidly and must be watched very closely. Finish the caramel by stopping the cooking with whatever liquid is called for in the recipe.

Caramel can be stored for months, either at room temperature or in the refrigerator, unless it is made with butter or cream, as in the rich caramel sauce on page 194. To clean the pan and dissolve any stuck-on caramel, either soak it in warm water or fill it with water and bring to a boil.

SOURCES

Sources for ingredients and equipment mentioned in this book are listed below. I have also included a few informational—and inspirational—Web sites and newsletters.

American Spoon Foods

411 East Cake Street
Petoskey, MI 49770
888-735-6700
www.spoon.com

Nuts, including wild hickory nuts, butternuts, and black walnuts, and specialty dried fruits, notably Montmorency sour cherries, which are terrific poached. The Web site includes an on-line catalog.

Amoretti

10021½ Canoga Avenue
Chatsworth, CA 91311
818-718-1239

Very fresh almond paste and other nut pastes, with no preservatives or artificial ingredients, freshly ground nut flours, and extracts of every possible variety.

Bridge Company

214 East 52nd Street
New York, NY 10022
212-688-4220
www.bridgekitchen.com

Great selection of baking supplies, knives, and pastry utensils for professionals and home cooks alike. The Web site includes an on-line catalog.

Chez Panisse

1517 Shattuck Avenue
Berkeley, CA 94709
www.chezpanisse.com

The Web site features facts about the restaurant café, including daily and weekly menus, and information about suppliers, ingredients, and sustainable agriculture, and the philosophy of founder Alice Waters and the Chez Panisse Foundation.

Guittard Chocolate Company

10 Guittard Road
Burlingame, CA 94010
800-769-1601
www.guittard.com

Although this company does not sell directly to the public, their Web site is full of information about their chocolate, including interesting facts about its production and tips on using it.

KCJ Vanilla Company

P.O. Box 126-ORD
Norwood, PA 19074

Bourbon, Tahitian, and Mexican vanilla extracts and beans, grown without pesticides, in single and double strengths.

King Arthur Flour Company
P.O. Box 876
Norwich, VT 05055-0876
800-827-6836
www.kingarthurflour.com

A great source for the avid baker. Ingredients available include flours (including tapioca flour), unsweetened coconut, and almond paste. A wide selection of cooling racks, Cambro food storage buckets, scales, baking sheets, and other baking supplies. Their Web site includes an on-line catalog.

Matfer
16249 Stagg Street
Van Nuys, CA 91406
800-766-0333

Pastry supplies and specialty baking equipment, mostly for professionals. The best whisks, sturdy composite plastic cutters, and piping tips. Exopat nonstick baking mats.

Parrish Decorating Supply
225 West 146th Street
Gardenia, CA 90248
800-736-8443

The best place to buy cake pans. Virtually every size, shape, and variety—all at reasonable prices.

Penzeys, Ltd.
P.O. Box 933
Muskego, WI 53150
414-679-7207
www.penzeys.com

Extensive selection of spices, including four varieties of cardamom, six varieties of cinnamon, both black and white poppy seeds, and three kinds of vanilla beans. Highly informative catalog and Web site.

Prévin
2044 Rittenhouse Square
Philadelphia, PA 19103
215-985-1996

Featuring bakeware, molds, cake pans, and specialty pastry supplies; primarily for professionals.

J. B. Prince
36 East 31st Street
New York, NY 10016
212-683-3553

Pastry supplies for professionals only. Many European items, including chocolate molds, reusable Silpat baking mats, and pastry books.

Professional Cutlery Direct
170 Boston Post Road, Suite 135
Madison, CT 06443
800-859-6994
www.cutlery.com

Very good selection of discounted quality cutlery and cookware. Their Web site includes an on-line catalog.

Pure Vanilla
Patricia Rain
P.O. Box 3206
Santa Cruz, CA 95063–3206
www.vanilla.com

Patricia Rain, "the queen of vanilla" and the author of *Vanilla Cookbook*, is a recognized expert on the subject. She specializes in vanilla products and vanilla information.

St. George Spirits
2900 Main Street
Alameda, CA 94501
www.stgeorgespirits.com

Jörg Rupf, a former attorney, distills eaux-de-vie and grappas that capture, with startling intensity, the essence of the best fruits available. I keep a bottle of his kirsch and Poire William (clear pear brandy) nearby when baking. Jörg also makes dessert wines from raspberries, pears, and varietal grapes. His Web site includes on-line ordering information.

Scharffen Berger Chocolate
250 South Maple Avenue C & F
South San Francisco, CA 94080
800-930-4528
www.Scharffen-Berger.com

Premium bittersweet and unsweetened chocolates and organic cocoa powder. The Web site contains information about chocolate, recipes, and on-line ordering.

Simple Cooking
John Thorne and Matt Lewis Thorne
P.O. Box 778
Northampton, MA 01061-0778
www.outlawcook.com

Excellent bimonthly food newsletter featuring John Thorne's reviews, recipes, and stories. Thorne writes thoughtful observations from a commonsense perspective and with an unabashed reverence for food.

Straus Family Creamery
P.O. Box 768
Marshall, CA 94940
www.strausmilk.com

One of the few certified organic dairies in the United States. Their heavy cream, sold in glass bottles, is the real thing—and tastes like it. Some of their products are available by mail order from their informative Web site.

Sur La Table
Catalog Division
1765 Sixth Avenue South
Seattle, WA 98134-1608
800-243-0852

Sur La Table carries a huge selection of cake pans, tart rings, molds, rolling pins, measuring cups and spoons, serving dishes, etc., etc., all meant for the serious home cook.

Sweet Celebrations
P.O. Box 39426
Edina, MN 55439-0426
800-328-6722

Catalog is filled with hard-to-find items: coarse crystal sugar, cake pans in a multitude of sizes, almond paste, Callebaut chocolate, white chocolate, edible rice paper (for panforte), candy cups and boxes, and candy-making equipment.

Tomales Bay Foods and
The Cowgirl Creamery
P.O. Box 594
Point Reyes Station, CA 94956
415-663-9335
www.cowgirlcreamery.com

Organic dairy products, including butter, crème fraîche, and handmade cheeses.

Williams–Sonoma
P.O. Box 7456
San Francisco, CA 94120
800-541-2233

Williams-Sonoma markets a well-selected assortment of baking supplies and cookware. For all the ice creams, sherbets, and sorbets in this book, I used a Williams-Sonoma ice cream maker with a self-contained freezing unit.

BIBLIOGRAPHY

Beranbaum, Rose Levy. *The Cake Bible.* New York: William Morrow, 1988.

Bernachon, Maurice, and Jean-Jacques Bernachon. *La Passion du Chocolat.* Paris: Flammarion, 1985.

Bianchini, Francesco, and Francesco Corbetta. *The Complete Book of Fruits and Vegetables.* New York: Crown, 1975.

Bilheux, Roland, and Alain Escoffier. *Professional French Pastry Series: Volume 1: Doughs, Batters, and Meringues.* New York: Van Nostrand Reinhold, 1988.

——. *Professional French Pastry Series: Volume 2: Creams, Confections, and Finished Desserts.* New York: Van Nostrand Reinhold, 1988.

——. *Professional French Pastry Series: Volume 3: Petits Fours, Chocolate, Frozen Desserts, and Sugar Work.* New York: Van Nostrand Reinhold, 1988.

Braker, Flo. *The Simple Art of Perfect Baking.* New York: William Morrow, 1985.

——. *Sweet Miniatures: The Art of Making Bite-Size Desserts.* New York: William Morrow, 1991.

Brennan, Georgeanne. *The Glass Pantry: The Pleasures of Simple Preserves.* San Francisco: Chronicle Books, 1994.

Commoli, Marianne, and Pierre Hermé. *Pierre Hermé, Pâtissier: Secrets Gourmands.* Paris: Larousse, 1994.

Corriher, Shirley O. *CookWise: The Hows and Whys of Successful Cooking.* New York: William Morrow, 1997.

Cost, Bruce. *Bruce Cost's Asian Ingredients: Buying and Cooking the Staple Foods of China, Japan, and Southeast Asia.* New York: William Morrow, 1988.

Cunningham, Marion. *The Fannie Farmer Baking Book.* New York: Alfred A. Knopf, 1984.

Damerow, Gail. *Ice Cream!: The Whole Scoop.* Macomb, Ill.: Glenbridge Publishing, 1991.

Field, Carol. *The Italian Baker.* New York: Harper & Row, 1985.

Gisslen, Wayne. *Professional Baking.* New York: John Wiley & Sons, 1985.

Grammatico, Maria, and Mary Taylor Simeti. *Bitter Almonds: Recollections and Recipes from a Sicilian Girlhood.* New York: William Morrow, 1994.

Grigson, Jane. *Jane Grigson's Fruit Book.* New York: Atheneum, 1982.

Healy, Bruce, and Paul Bugat. *Mastering the Art of French Pastry: An Illustrated Course.* Woodbury, N.Y.: Barron's, 1984.

Hedrick, U. P. *The Small Fruits of New York.* Albany, N.Y.: J. B. Lyon, 1925.

Jones, Judith, and Evan Jones. *The L.L. Bean Book of New New England Cookery.* New York: Random House, 1987.

Kander, Mrs. Simon. *The Settlement Cookbook.* New York: Simon & Schuster, 1951.

Lanza, Anna Tasca. *The Flavors of Sicily.* New York: Clarkson N. Potter, 1996.

Lenôtre, Gaston. *Lenôtre's Desserts and Pastries.* Woodbury, N.Y.: Barron's, 1977.

Let's Sell Ice Cream. Washington, D.C.: The Ice Cream Merchandising Institute, 1947.

Luchetti, Emily. *Four-Star Desserts.* New York: HarperCollins, 1996.

Lyle, Katie Letcher. *The Wild Berry Book: Romance, Recipes & Remedies.* Minocqua, Wis.: NorthWord, 1994.

Malgieri, Nick. *How to Bake.* New York: HarperCollins, 1995.

McGee, Harold. *On Food and Cooking: The Science and Lore of the Kitchen.* New York: Charles Scribner's Sons, 1984.

Medrich, Alice. *Chocolate and the Art of Low-Fat Desserts.* New York: Warner Books, 1994.

———. *Cocolat: Extraordinary Chocolate Desserts.* New York: Warner Books, 1990.

Meis, John Dore. *A Taste of Tuscany.* New York: Abbeville, 1993.

Mercier, Jacques. *Belgian Chocolate: Pralines, Batons, Desserts, Biscuits . . .* Belgium: La Renaissance du Livre, 1997.

Ortiz, Gayle, and Joe Ortiz, with Louisa Beers. *The Village Baker's Wife: The Desserts and Pastries That Made Gayle's Famous.* Berkeley, Calif.: Ten Speed Press, 1997.

Pellaprat, Henri-Paul. *Modern French Culinary Art.* Cleveland: World Publishing Company, 1966.

Rain, Patricia. *Vanilla Cookbook.* Berkeley, Calif.: Celestial Arts, 1986.

Rombauer, Irma S., with Marion Rombauer Becker and Ethan Becker. *Joy of Cooking.* New York: Scribner, 1997.

Rosso, Julee, and Sheila Lukins, with Michael McLaughlin. *The Silver Palate Cookbook.* New York: Workman, 1979.

Sax, Richard. *Classic Home Desserts: A Treasury of Heirloom and Contemporary Recipes from Around the World.* Shelburne, Vt.: Chapters Publishing, 1994.

Schneider, Elizabeth. *Uncommon Fruits and Vegetables: A Commonsense Guide.* New York: Harper & Row, 1986.

Shere, Lindsey Remolif. *Chez Panisse Desserts.* New York: Random House, 1985.

Silverton, Nancy. *Desserts by Nancy Silverton*. New York: Harper & Row, 1986.

Stearn, William T., and Frederick A. Roach. *Hooker's Finest Fruits: A Selection of Paintings of Fruits by William Hooker (1779–1832)*. New York: Prentice Hall, 1989.

Stewart, Martha. *Martha Stewart's Pies and Tarts*. New York: Clarkson N. Potter, 1985.

Susser, Allen. *The Great Citrus Book*. Berkeley, Calif.: Ten Speed Press, 1997.

Waters, Alice. *Chez Panisse Menu Cookbook*. New York: Random House, 1982.

Whealy, Kent, and Steve Demuth, eds. *Fruit, Berry and Nut Inventory, Second Edition: An Inventory of Nursery Catalogs Listing All Fruit, Berry and Nut Varieties Available by Mail Order in the United States*. Decorah, Iowa: Seed Saver Publications, 1993.

INDEX

G

galette:
    apple and frangipane, 81
    dough, 186
gâteau victoire, 32
gelatin, 10
gelato, chocolate, 125
gelées:
    Champagne, with citrus
        fruits and kumquats,
        130–31
    red wine, with peaches, 133
    sorbets, sherbets, ice
        creams and, 104–33
ginger:
    candied, 165
    fresh, cake, 44
    fresh, nectarines baked
        with pistachios and, 93
    pineapple marmalade, 175
    in tropical fruit soup, 102–3
    –white chocolate ice
        cream with chocolate-
        covered peanuts,
        122–23
gingersnaps, 144–45
grape, Concord:
    "jelly," 132
    pie, 84
grapefruit peel, in variation
        of candied orange
        peel, 166

grapefruits, 14
    in Champagne gelée with
        citrus fruits and
        kumquats, 130–31
graters, 5
grenadine, in variation of soft
        candied citrus peel, 197
grinders, spice, 6
Guittard Chocolate
        Company, 203

H

Hazan, Marcella, 125
hazelnuts:
    in marjolaine, 28–31
    in panforte, 160–61
hickory nuts, wild, butterscotch
        ice cream with, 127
honey:
    and Chartreuse, mint
        sherbet with warm
        figs in, 116
    in frozen nougat, 128–29
    nougat, 162
    in panforte, 160–61
huckleberry(ies):
    plum upside-down
        cake, 38–39
    in variation of blueberry
        compote, 97

I

ice cream freezers, 6
ice creams:
    butterscotch, with wild
        hickory nuts, 127
    caramel, 124
    Mexican chocolate, 126
    sorbets, sherbets, gelées
        and, 104–33
    vanilla, 121
    white chocolate–ginger,
        with chocolate-covered
        peanuts, 122–23
ingredients, 7–10

J

jam:
    fig, 178
    plum strawberry, 177
"jelly," Concord grape, 132
Jordan, Julie, x
Joy of Cooking (Rombauer,
        Rombauer Becker, and
        Becker), 170
juicers, 6

K

KCJ Vanilla Company, 203
King Arthur Flour
    Company, 204
kirsch:
    in blackberry sorbet, 108
    in blueberry and white
        chocolate tart, 98–99
    in pineapple, rhubarb and
        raspberry cobbler, 88–89
    in plum raspberry
        compote, 96
    in summer pudding, 94
knives, 5
kumquats, 14
    and citrus fruits,
        Champagne gelée
        with, 130–31
    sugared, 168

L

ladles, 3
lemon, Meyer:
    semifreddo, 40–41
    sorbet, 111
lemon peel, in variation
        of candied orange
        peel, 166
lemons, 14

lime(s), 15
    in Champagne gelée with
        citrus fruits and
        kumquats, 130–31
    in tropical tiramisù, 46–47
liqueurs, 170–73
    nocino, 173
    vin d'orange, 172
loganberries, in variation
        of plum raspberry
        compote, 96

M

macadamia chocolate cake, 33
macaroons, coconut, 152
mango(es), 15
    sauce, 199
    strawberry sorbet, 109
    in tropical tiramisù, 46–47
maple walnut–pear cake,
        42–43
marjolaine, 28–31
marmalade:
    pineapple ginger, 175
    Seville orange, 176
Matfer, 204
measuring cups and spoons, 2
meringues:
    in marjolaine, 28–31
    in Pavlova, 100–101
    in tropical fruit soup, 102–3

metal spatulas, 3
Mexican chocolate
        ice cream, 126
Mexican wedding cookies, 154
Meyer lemon(s), 14
    semifreddo, 40–41
    sorbet, 111
milk, 8
mills, food, 2
mint sherbet with warm figs
        in Chartreuse and
        honey, 116
mixers, electric, 2
mixing bowls, 3
Monsoon, viii, xii, 69, 102, 120,
        132, 142, 165

N

nectarine(s), 15
    baked with pistachios and
        fresh ginger, 93
    white, sorbet with black-
        berries in plum wine
        in a five-spice cookie
        cup, 114–15
nocino, 173
    custard, 56
nougat:
    frozen, 128–29
    honey, 162
nut jobs, chocolate
        almond, 159

nuts, 9–10
  in chocolate chunk
    cookies, 137
  spiced candied, 163
  see also specific nuts

O

olallieberries, in variation
    of plum raspberry
    compote, 96
orange(s), 16
  almond bread pudding, 68
  caramel sauce, 195
  cardamom flan, 61–62
  in Champagne gelée
    with citrus fruits and
    kumquats, 130–31
  in pineapple ginger
    marmalade, 175
  –poppy seed cookies,
    148–49
  sesame almond tuiles, 156
  Seville, marmalade, 176
  vin d', 172
orange peel, candied, 166

P

panforte, 160–61
pans, cake, 5
papaya, in variation of tropical
    tiramisù, 46–47

parchment paper, 4
Parrish Decorating Supply, 204
passion fruit, 16
  pound cake, 48–49
  sorbet, 107
  in variation of tropical
    tiramisù, 46–47
paste, quince, 169
pastry brushes, 4
pastry cream, 189
pâte à choux, 187
pavé, chocolate, 26–27
Pavlova, 100–101
peaches, 16–17
  red wine gelée with, 133
  in variation of nectarines
    baked with pistachios
    and fresh ginger, 93
peanut butter cookies, 142
peanuts, chocolate-covered,
    white chocolate–ginger
    ice cream with, 122–23
pear(s), 17
  –maple-walnut cake, 42–43
  rum, and pecan tart, 76–77
  very spicy caramel, 73
pecan(s):
  –brown sugar
    shortbread, 146
  in Mexican wedding
    cookies, 154
  pear and rum tart, 76–77
  tuiles, 155

in variation of chocolate
    almond nut jobs, 159
in variation of red banana
    soufflé, 66–67
peelers, vegetable, 5
Penzeys, Ltd., 204
persimmon(s), 17–18
  cake, 37
pie plates and weights, 6
pies:
  banana butterscotch
    cream, 86–87
  butternut squash, 92
  Concord grape, 84
  dough, 184–85
Pilgram, Gilbert, 126
pineapple(s), 18
  ginger marmalade, 175
  rhubarb, and raspberry
    cobbler, 88–89
  in tropical tiramisù, 46–47
pistachio(s):
  and cardamom cake with
    apricots poached in
    Sauternes, 35–36
  in frozen nougat, 128–29
  in honey nougat, 162
  nectarines baked with
    fresh ginger and, 93
  in variation of chocolate
    macadamia cake, 33
plastic containers, 3
plates, pie, 6